Robert Elliott Speer

Missions and Politics in Asia

Studies of the Spirit of the Eastern Peoples, the Present Making of History in Asia

Robert Elliott Speer

Missions and Politics in Asia
Studies of the Spirit of the Eastern Peoples, the Present Making of History in Asia

ISBN/EAN: 9783744757171

Printed in Europe, USA, Canada, Australia, Japan

Cover: Foto ©Suzi / pixelio.de

More available books at **www.hansebooks.com**

STUDENTS' LECTURES ON MISSIONS
Princeton Theological Seminary
M DCCC XCVIII

Missions and Politics in Asia

Studies of the spirit of the Eastern peoples, the present making of history in Asia, and the part therein of Christian Missions

BY

ROBERT E. SPEER

Secretary of the Presbyterian Board of Foreign Missions

New York   Chicago   Toronto
Fleming H. Revell Company
M DCCC XCVIII

TO THE MISSIONARIES
IN HAMADAN, PERSIA

Preface

THE lectures composing this volume were suggested by the studies and observation of an extended tour in Asia, in the years 1896 and 1897. They are printed substantially as they were delivered to the faculty and students of Princeton Theological Seminary in February, 1898. Their object was to sketch in broad outline the spirit of the Eastern peoples, the present making of history in Asia and the part therein of Christian Missions. They are at once the fruit and the ground of the conviction, vindicated by the obvious facts of history and of life, that Christ is the present Lord and King of all life and history and their certain goal.

Contents

LECTURE I—PERSIA   13

THE PRESENT POLITICS OF ASIA. Its interest. Ancient Persia. Zoroastrianism. The Arab conquest. Its results. The origin of Shiahism. Its doctrines. Relation of Church and State in Persia unlike their relation in Turkey. The doctrine of the Imam. The Babis. Reactions against Shiahism. The Sufis. Omar Khayam. The Wahabis. The present situation. The condition of religion: (1) Its moral fruits; (2) Its political failure. The utter ruin of the country and its religion. The forces shaping the future: (1) Political; (2) Missionary. History. Grounds of toleration. The non-Moslem peoples. The character of the missionaries.

LECTURE II—SOUTHERN ASIA   67

BAGDAD. Turkish rule. (1) It is corrupt and should be ended. (2) Its oppression of Christians. (3) Its dependence upon Christian Nations for existence. (4) Dismal prospect. (5) Feebleness of the Mission force. Arabia. The influence of Aden. The problem of India. The situation. (1) The want of Indian unity at the time of the British conquest. (2) The conditions and character of the conquest. (3) The unification of India under British influence, and the great perils thereof. (4) England's failure to guard against these in her education of India. (5) This failure in a measure atoned for by Missions. Their great power and influence. Indo-China and Buddhism.

LECTURE III—CHINA   119

THE CHARACTER OF THE CHINESE. Burlingame's view of it. Its greatness. Its idiosyncrasy. Its impressiveness. How has it been produced? The isolation of the Chinese. The education of the Chinese. The civil service. Confucianism. The attitude of China toward outside nations. The contact of China and the West. The opening of the country. The nature and result of its foreign intercourse since. The situation hopeless so far as concerns (1) the Chinese religions. (2) China's political and civil instituticns. (3) Western trade and diplomacy. Hope in Christian Missions. Their history in China. Their obstacles. (1) The difficulty of adjustment to the Chinese mind. (2) Political entanglements. Mr. Norman's criticism and condemnation of Missions.

Contents

Lecture IV—Japan 169

THE CONTRAST WITH CHINA. Japan's historic debt to China. Original features of Japanese civilization. Contact with the West. Three stages of Japanese history since Perry's visit. "Foreign intercourse" the directing principle. Different courses of Japan and China. The forces moulding Japan. The place of Christianity in shaping the new institutions. The present temper of the people. (1) Industrialism. (2) National pride. (3) Militarism. (4) Nationalism and foreign antagonism. (5) Moral bewilderment and irreligiousness. The course and effect of the Christian movement. The defects of the Japanese. The prospect hopeful.

Lecture V—Korea 219

THE EASTWARD MOVEMENT OF THE EASTERN QUESTION. Its location in Korea. The historic relations of Korea to China and Japan. The opening of Korea to other nations. The part of Missions therein. Roman Catholic Missions. America's relations to Korea. Japan's part in unlocking the land. The causes of the China-Japan war. The Tong Haks. The sequel of the war. Russia's unearned prize. The political situation. The place and influence of the Korean Church. Its patriotism. The outlook. Conclusion. The bearing of such a study as this upon Mission method. Its dangers. Its bearing on Mission motive. The Kingdom of God the goal.

LECTURE I

Persia

Persia, that imaginary seat of Oriental splendor! that land of poets and roses! that cradle of mankind, that uncontaminated source of Eastern manners lay before me. . . . I will not say that all my dreams were realized; for perhaps no country in the world less comes up to one's expectations than Persia,—whether in the beauties of nature, or the riches and magnificence of its inhabitants. . . .

A distinct line must ever be drawn between " the nations who wear the hat and those who wear the beard"; and they must ever hold each other's stories improbable, until a more general intercourse of common life takes place between them. What is moral and virtuous with the one, is wickedness with the other,—what the Christian reviles as abominable, is by the Mohammedan held sacred. Although the contrast between their respective manners may be very amusing, still it is most certain that the former will ever feel devoutly grateful that he is neither subject to the Mohammedan rule, nor educated in Mohammedan principles; whilst the latter, in his turn, looking upon the rest of mankind as unclean infidels, will continue to hold fast to his bigoted persuasion until some powerful interposition of Providence shall dispel the moral and intellectual darkness which, at present, overhangs so large a portion of the Asiatic world.

JAMES MORIER, *Hajji Baba of Ispahan.*

LECTURE I

PERSIA

"Praise be to God, the Lord of all creatures; the most merciful, the king of the day of judgment. Thee do we worship, and of thee do we beg assistance. Direct us in the right way, in the way of those to whom thou hast been gracious; not of those against whom thou art incensed, nor of those who go astray." Though not chronologically first, this is the opening Sura of the Koran,[1] and it is the characteristic note of the noblest assertion ever made by man of the sovereignty of God, and of His lordship over human history,—"The Lord of all creatures. . . . The king of the day of judgment . . . the most high; who hath created and completely formed His creatures; and who determineth them to various ends and directeth them to attain the same" (Sura lxvii.). And the words with which the Koran begins, suggest the thought which will give shape and bounds to what will be said in these lectures. I believe in the Lord, the living, the powerful, in whose hand our life is, and by

[1] Sale's *Koran*, chap. I.

Missions and Politics

whom the courses of men and of nations are shaped, as in the East the water brooks are turned by the husbandman whithersoever he will. And I wish to trace briefly the play of the forces that are now working out in Asia the designs of God.

For great history is making in the East, no longer unchangeable. Its life is astir with new movement. The old forms are not gone. They linger still with strong tenacity, vitalized often by the touch of the new influences; but the tides that swept out of Asia thirty centuries ago, purified, filled with new energy, "turn again home." And as they wake the old peoples to a new youth, a fresh chapter of human history begins. We call it only politics, as these forces lock in Asia. But "politics," as Mr. Freeman said "is present history, and history is past politics."

No history has ever been greater than that which is making now. Our times are prosaic only to men of prosaic minds. The romance which hangs over Cyrus and Darius and Artaxerxes, over Jenghiz Khan and his sons, and that great city where

> " Alph, the sacred river ran
> Through caverns measureless to man
> Down to a sunless sea,"

Persia

over Saracen, Mogul and Sikh; Khaled, Akbar and Runjit Singh, is as the play of children beside the stern struggle of our own day in Asia. Systems of thought and morals and social custom which were old before we were peoples, and which have set themselves never to be moved, have been challenged and shaken. Commerce, diplomacy, civilization have violated their repose. Righteousness has demanded a reckoning of them. And Christianity, of which these are the children, is calmly confronting them from foundations which cannot be removed, while new foundations are laid for her on their enlarging ruins. It is a privilege to live with open eyes in the age of such a conflict, to watch the movements of the struggle, to hear the tumult of the chariots and the horsemen, and to discern in all, the master hand of the Lord, "the Lord of all creatures, the King of the day of judgment . . . who determineth His creatures to various ends and directeth them to attain the same." It is better than "a crush of worlds."

For out of this struggle a new earth is coming. What we are watching are not so much death gasps as birth throes,—the pangs of a mighty labor on the old mother Asia. And I believe that what she has borne is naught in comparison with

Missions and Politics

what she is yet to bear. That it is a constructive, a creative time some may fail to see who are "blind, unable to discern that which is afar off" (2 Peter i. 9). But if our eyes are opened, we shall see

> "The new age that stands as yet,
> Half built against the sky,
> Open to every threat
> Of storms that clamor by :
> While scaffolding veils the walls,
> And dim dust floats and falls,
> As moving to and fro, their tasks the masons ply."

With this idea dominating our thought, I propose to speak to-day of Persia and Islam, judging that the view of which I have spoken will exclude nothing that is of human interest.

Of what Persia was before she fell under Islam it is not necessary to speak. The days of her glory and world-dominion are far, far off from the poor political ruin of to-day, and the powers that made her greatness were spent long before the Chosrœs succeeded to the power of the Achemenians, the Seleucidæ, the Arsacidæ and the Sassanians and the long struggle with Heraclius had drained the land of its energy and resources. The Persia with which we deal to-day is the product of the Mohammedan conquest and we need not go beyond that for an understanding of it.

Persia

It was in the seventh century that the Arabian armies poured up from the Southwest into the Mesopotamian plains to finish the work that the Roman Emperor Heraclius had begun, and to open the last chapter of the great degeneracy. I commend to you the romance of that great tragedy as it is set forth in Muir's *Annals of the Early Caliphate*. Just one year ago we rode over the hills and valleys and plains where this struggle between the last of the Chosrœs and the generals of Mohammed and Omar surged to and fro, yet pressed ever Eastward. It was a wonderful battleground. Every farsakh of the weary way was eloquent with appeal from the great past to the armies of Yezdegird. Over this road Cyrus and Darius had led their hosts. On the craggy cliffs of Beseitun past which the Saracens drove the Persians, were the inscriptions of Darius, telling of his world-wide victories, and showing to the desperate troops as they passed, the giant figure with his foot on the neck of a captive, and his subjugated foes chained throat to throat before him. Yet cut on the rocks below, were the name of Alexander and royal figures plain enough then to remind the fugitives that ten centuries before another conquerer had possessed their land. The mounds and the temples of their fire-worship rose here and there in the plains. They looked back as they fled upon the glorious white stone palace at Kasr-i-shirin, and saw the rough Arabs plunder its beauties. One evening, just one year ago, as the sun was setting behind hills all purple and saffron, save as they were white-crested with snow, we stood in the ruins of this noble palace, and saw again the old days when it had stood as

"A dwelling of kings, ere the world was waxen old.
   Dukes were the doorwards there, and the roof was thatched with gold."

And I thought how the gleam of it must have been as the farewell of the past to Yezdegird. Up through the passes and over the Zagros ranges they fled, until on the plains of Nehavend, under the pure, white peaks of Elvend, and across the hills from Ecbatana, in 641, the decisive issue was joined and Omar's captain Nowan sent word back to his master that Persia was the Prophet's.

The first fruit of the Arab conquest was the destruction of Zoroastrianism. There were some admirable things in Zoroastrianism. "It ascribed no immoral attributes to the object of worship. . . . It sanctioned no immoral acts as a part of worship. None of the prescribed forms of worship is marked by cruelty. In the great contest between light and darkness, the Avesta exhorts the true worshipper not to remain passive, but to contend with all his might against the productions of the Evil Principle. There is an absence of image worship, and the Avesta never despairs of the future of humanity; it affirms the final victory of good over evil."[1] But all this and vastly more could be said of Mohammedanism, and that vigorous and uncompromising system swept up against the old Persian religion like a storm and well-nigh obliterated it. There are eight times as many Parsis now in the Bombay Presidency as there are in the land of their origin. In Persia there are less than 10,000 of them; a few in Teheran, where the Tower of Silence near ancient Rhei is still the place of exposure of their dead, but most of them in Kirman and at Yezd, where there are said to be four altars which keep alive the sacred flame, as Moore recalls in his line,

"Yezd's eternal mansion of the fire."

There are elements of fire-worship in the rites of the Ali Illahees, an heretical and eclectic Moslem sect that has enrolled Henry Martyn and David Livingstone among its avatars, and whose sacrament is a communion of fire eating. And there are traces of the old worship of the sun in private

[1] Mitchell's *Zend Avesta and the Religion of the Parsis*, p. 49.

Missions and Politics

and common life. It is customary in many places when a light is brought into a room, to salute it as we would a person, while in the cities where members of the royal Kajar family reside, the old Kajar music sounding like a callithumpian serenade bursts forth from some royal palace at the rising or the setting of the sun. The few Zoroastrians who remain are under as grievous disabilities as the Christians, however. The stern, relentless faith of the Prophet made clean work and did not play with compromise.

The second fruit of the Arab conquest was the destruction of independence. For nine centuries, Saracen, Tartar and Turkish dynasties, all alien, ruled over the land. It was not a barren period. The hearts of the subject people were cheered by Firdousi, Hafiz and Omar Khayam; and Avicenna, whose tomb is still in good repair at Hamadan, gave Persia a name for medical science. When in these centuries, however, hope ever kindled, it kindled but to be swept away by some new dynasty, or by the unique triumphs of Jenghis Khan and his sons, or Tamerlane, until in the fifteenth century, a political movement grew out of the Sunnee-Shiah controversy, which ended in the independence of Persia.

Persia

An understanding of this controversy is essential to any insight into Persian history since the Arab invasions, and also to an appreciation of the present and future developments of both religion and politics in Turkey, Persia and India.

The Shiah schism arose in the early days of Islam. The name Shiah means sectaries.[1] Mohammedanism has never been really one. It seems strange, as Sale suggests, that Spinoza, even if ignorant of the general fact of its multitudinous heresies, should have been ignorant of this notorious division, and should "have assigned as the reason for preferring the order of the Mohammedan Church to that of the Roman, that there have arisen no schisms in the former since its birth." The same error is frequently made, however, in our own day. The unity of Islam is often held up as a rebuke to divided Christendom. But Mohammedans would not be grateful for this conspicuousness. They say "The Magians are divided into seventy sects, the Jews into seventy-one, the Christians into seventy-two, and the Moslems into seventy-three, as Mohammed had foretold." Even in schism Islam claims precedence. Moreover its devotees have passed beyond Christendom in

[1] Benjamin's *Persia and the Persians*, Boston Ed., 1887, chaps. xii., xiii.

Missions and Politics

this, that only one sect is entitled to salvation in their view, each sect holding the others damnable. Historically almost innumerable sects have been developed, of which the Sunnees and Shiahs with their subdivisions, and the Matazalites, the Safatians and Kharejites were the principal.

The origin of their sect explains something of the deep and patriotic devotion of the Shiahs to their heroes. The breech with the orthodox body arose out of a civil war. Ali, the cousin of Mohammed, married his daughter Fatima, and was the fourth caliph of Islam, Othman, Omar and Abu Bekr intervening between him and the Prophet. Sell quotes the description which pictures him as "the last and worthiest of the primitive Mussulmans who imbibed his religious enthusiasm from companionship with the Prophet himself, and who followed to the last the simplicity of his character;" and adds, "He was a man calculated by his earnest devotion to the Prophet and his own natural graces to win, as he has done, the admiration of succeeding generations." Factional contentions came to an issue in his caliphate, however, and he was assassinated in a mosque at Kufa. One of his two sons, Hasan, relinquished his claim to the succes-

Persia

sion to Muavia, who had been his father's rival. To get Hasan out of the way, however, he was poisoned by his own wife. Muavia's son succeeded him, and saw the house of Ali destroyed in his second son, Hussein, who was slain near Kerbela, where the enemy killed off his small band of companions until he and his little son alone were left. The little boy was slain by an arrow which pierced his ear. "We came from God and we return to Him," said the grandson of the Prophet, and kneeling down to drink of the Euphrates, was struck with an arrow in the mouth, and fell forward wounded with many wounds. And thus was the great schism born.[1]

From that day to this, Sunnee and Shiah have had only hate for one another. "Who is that?" we asked our Persian servant, as a large Turk passed through our courtyard at Khanikin, on the Turkish side of the frontier. "One dog," was the laconic reply. "Englishman good," said the same man later, "Persian fair, Osmanli foul." "Whoso goes over the border," say the Persians of Ardalan, "goes under the ground." Each year the fast of Moharrem keeps alive in Shiah breasts the memories of the wrongs of the

[1] Sell's *Faith of Islam*, Ed., 1880, pp. 73, 74.

Missions and Politics

house of Ali. Readers relate the story of the tragedies. Flagellants, dripping with blood and lacerated with scorpions, cry aloud with grief, and the multitudes looking on bewail the foul treacheries, and heat to fresh passion the long fostered hate of the Sunnee.[1] Each year thousands and tens of thousands flock to Kerbela, not far from Babylon and Bagdad, to worship at the shrine of the martyred Hussein, and to bury the bones of their dead in the sacred soil.

The chief points of difference between the Sunnees and Shiahs cannot be better summarized than in the statement of Sale,[2] "1. That the Shiahs reject Abu Bekr, Omar and Othman, the first three caliphs, as usurpers and intruders; whereas the Sunnees acknowledge and respect them as rightful Imams. 2. The Shiahs prefer Ali to Mohammed, or at least esteem the two equal; but the Sunnees admit neither Ali nor any of the prophets to be equal to Mohammed. 3. The Sunnees charge the Shiahs with corrupting the Koran and neglecting its precepts, and the Shiahs retort the same charge on the Sunnees. 4. The Sunnees receive the Sunna (whence their name) or book of traditions of their Prophet, as

---
[1] Benjamin's *Persia and the Persians*, Boston Ed., chap. xiii.
[2] Sale's *Koran*, Prelim. Discourse, sec. viii.

Persia

of canonical authority; whereas the Shiahs reject it as apocryphal and unworthy of credit."

Dropping out of comparison for an instant, the Sunnee belief, a precise statement of the fundamental tenets of Shiahism would include: belief in the unity of God; belief in the divine mission of all the prophets, and, that Mohammed is the chief of all; the admissions that God is just, and that Ali is next in order after Mohammed, that Ali's descendants from Hasan to Mahdi, the twelfth Imam, are his true successors, and that all of them in character, position and dignity are raised far above all other Moslems.

The Persians early became adherents of the Shiah sect.[1] For centuries they were ruled over by Sunnee kings. The religious breach constantly widened. Their old Arab conquerors were also members of the Sunnee body. At the very close of the fifteenth century, the Sunnee yoke was broken, and Ismail established the Sefavean dynasty, which was both Shiah and Persian. Under his fourth successor, Shah Abbas, the Great, who ascended the throne in 1586, Persia rose into golden days again. The vitality of the people which had never been wholly crushed, rallied, and bridges, caravan-

---
[1] Haines's *Islam as a Missionary Religion*, p. 66.

saries and countless ruins are now traced back by the people to Shah Abbas. Mohammed, an Afghan, overthrew the Sefavean dynasty in 1722, but fell in 1727 before Nadir, a Persian soldier, who proclaimed himself king, defeated the Turks, conquered Afghanistan, captured Delhi, married his son to the daughter of the Mogul Emperor in India, and came back with the famous peacock throne to Teheran. The present dynasty of Kajars, Shiahs but not Persians, Turks rather from the Northeast, and not of Osmanli stock, was set up by Agha Mohammed Khan in 1794. The Kajars have probably done as much for Persia as any dynasty could that might have been native to the soil, but they have been, and this is a vital point, in nowise related to the line of Ali.

Let us note the bearing of these two facts:—first, that the Persians are Shiahs, and second, that their ruling dynasty is non-Imamic, i. e., not of the line of Ali, upon the political and religious conditions of Asia, and indeed upon the whole Eastern Question.

The chief point to be noted is, that the Shiahs believe Ali to have been lawful caliph and Imam, and hold that the supreme authority in all things spiritual and temporal, State no less than Church,

Persia

of right belongs to his descendants. Their devotion to Ali exceeds all bounds. In one of the sanctuaries of the great mosque at Kum, which is the Westminster Abbey of Persia, is this inscription to him, "Oh, inexpressible man! By thee in truth is nature enriched and adorned! Had not thy perfect self been in the Creator's thought, Eve had remained forever a virgin and Adam a bachelor." Now Ali's descendants enjoy no such rights in Persia as the tenets of Shiahism claim for them. The civil power is in the hands of the Kajar dynasty, and the Kajars are in nowise connected with Ali. According to the strict faith of the Shiahs, they are usurpers of authority belonging to Ali's descendants, in whose hands is the ecclesiastical power. There is, accordingly, a real separation between Church and State in Persia, more real in some senses than exists in France or England or Germany or Russia. In Islam, using the word in its popular sense, such a condition as this is a logical contradiction. Mohammed's Islam, the Islam of the caliphs was the State. It grew by appealing to those motives which only civil power could satisfy, and by making such promises as only as a political and military organization Islam could fulfill. Deprived of the power of appealing to such motives and of making such promises, and reduced to a religion merely, Islam ceases to be Islam. To this condition Persian Mohammedanism is practically reduced. It is only a religion. It is the established religion. The State does for it some things which Christian States with established religions do not do for them; but it does not subsidize it financially as some Christian States do. But Mohammedanism cannot endure, robbed of its political character. It may become a modified, modernized Islam, a surrender to the fate of God; but it will not be the old fiery, irresistible tempest that burst out of Arabia and shook the nations. It will have to take its place among the world's religions, not as a political institution, but as a system of morals and faith. This is practically what it has had to do in Persia. It controls the passage of property, and still possesses many political advantages including a good share of the judiciary functions of government, but it has been in conflict rather than in partnership with the Kajar dynasty.[1] The civil power has by no means triumphed over it. There are even indications that the present Shah may surrender something of what his father had gained in his

---

[1] Benjamin's *Persia and the Persians*, Boston Ed., 1887, chap. xv.

Persia

long conflict with the Mollahs. But Islam has been obliged radically to change its character, and Shiah Mohammedanism must become less and less like the Mohammedanism of Abu Bekr and the world conquering caliphs, and more and more a religion simply, with no appeal save to the conscience and intellect of man, perhaps rather to his fanaticism and bigotry.

It will be seen, therefore, that even if the Shiah ecclesiastics should wish to enter into compact with the Turks or with the Mohammedans of India to establish a united Islam, with which to confront the encroachments of the Christian Nations upon the last strongholds of the Faith, they would be unable to deliver the Persian civil power to such a league. There is but little likelihood of their desire, however, to enter into union or compact with the Sunnees. Their differences are too great. They blame the present Sunnees for the slaughter of Ali and his sons. They charge the present Sunnees with usurpation. And they are the more alienated by the device by which the Turk has saved Sunnee Mohammedanism from the mortal separation of the civil and ecclesiastical power which has befallen the Mohammedanism of the Shiahs, and of the way this device collides with the most vital and precious principle

Missions and Politics

of the Shiahs, namely their doctrine of their Imam or Spiritual and Absolute Head.

In Turkey, the head of Church and State is one. The Sultan is also the caliph. It is clearly laid down in Mohammedan law that the caliph must be of the tribe of the Koreish, to which the Prophet belonged. And Abdul Hamid is neither Koreish nor Arab at all, but he claims the caliphate. It came about in this way. After the dismal end of the Abbassid dynasty of caliphs in Bagdad in 1258, a mock caliphate was set up and maintained in Egypt. When Selim I., Sultan of the Osmanli Turks conquered Egypt in 1516, the mock caliphate came to an end, and Muttawakkil Billal, the last of the puppet caliphs of Egypt, and a descendant from the thirty-fifth caliph of Bagdad, surrendered his supposed rights to Suleiman, the successor of Selim. So to this day the Osmanli sultans, of whom Abdul Hamid is the thirty-fourth, have claimed to be the spiritual as well as the political successors of Mohammed. The claim is a poor dream. The Arabs and Moors scorn it.[1] The Hindus mock at it, and the Persians detest it. Those apologists for England's inactivity during the Armenian massacres, and her breach of faith with the simple people for whom she had sol-

---
[1] Muir's *Caliphate*, London Ed., 1892, pp. 589-594.

Persia

emnly bound herself by the treaty of Berlin, whose terms she had dictated, to secure reforms, on the ground that her hostility toward the Sultan would lead to an uprising in India, were deceived. The India Mohammedans are not partisans of the Sultan, nor do they recognize the validity of the fiction by which he claims to be not only civil head of the Osmanli State, but also spiritual head of the Mohammedan Church.

But most of all do the Persian Shiahs reject the idea, because it collides with their loyalty to Ali, and their favorite doctrine of the Imam. The word Imam comes from an Arabic word meaning to aim at, to follow after, and signifies accordingly, leader or exemplar. Mohammed of course was the first great leader. Then came Ali, and the Shiahs hold that the leadership, the Imamat, must continue in and be confined to his line, and that the whole essence of religion is devotion to the rightful Imam. A Persian hymn shows the depth of this sentiment toward Ali and the Imams:

> "Mysterious being! none can tell
> The attributes in thee that dwell;
> None can thine essence comprehend;
> To thee should every mortal bend—
> For 'tis by thee that man is given
> To know the high behests of heaven."

Missions and Politics

The Shiahs hold that "the Imam is the successor of the Prophet, adorned with all the qualities which he possessed, wiser than the most learned men of the age, holier than the most pious; free from all sin original and active. His authority is the authority of God." His body is so pure and delicate as to cast no shadow. He is the supreme pontiff, the vicar of God on earth. "The Koran, the infallible book, is plussed by the Imam, the infallible man."[1]

On this doctrine of the Imam the Shiahs are divided into two parties. I speak of them because they also serve to explain modern history and the movement of Christianity in Asia and Africa. The Imamites reckoning Ali as the first, believe in twelve Imams, the last of whom Abul Kasim, is still alive, though concealed, and bears the name of Al Mahdi, "the guided." The Ismailians believe that since the sixth Imam, the Imams have been concealed. The Imam is in existence now, but concealed. There are always those who say, "Next year the Mahdi will appear." There is fine soil in this belief for a crop of disturbances and small fanaticisms of which we have not seen the last. It explains many things about Moslem lands, and makes move-

[1] Sell's *Faith of Islam*, Edition, 1880, pp. 76, 78.

Persia

ments like modern Babism intelligible. The founder of this sect, Mirza Ali Mohammed, the Bab, was the son of a Shiraz grocer, born in 1819 or 1820. His manifestation as a prophet was in 1844 at Bushire. His name of Bab, or gate, signified his claim to be the one through whom alone knowledge of the twelfth Imam Mahdi could be attained. His pretensions grew apace and he soon advanced himself as the Mahdi, then as a re-incarnation of the Prophet, then as a Revelation or Incarnation of God Himself. The Bab was shot at Tabriz in 1850, and the Babis, his followers, removed to Bagdad. Thence the Turkish government removed them to Constantinople and then to Adrianople in 1866. One of them Mirza Hussein Ali, or Beha, announced himself as the Mahdi, whom the Bab had foretold. This led to a dissension and bloody schism, ending in the permanent division of the Babis, with two prophets, Beha at Acre, and his younger brother at Cyprus, where the British government pensioned him. There are now supposed to be between half a million and a million Babis in Persia, nineteen-twentieths of them Behais, or of the Beha party. In spite of martyrdom and the fiercest persecution the sect has grown, until now its leader having given it a

Missions and Politics

dispensation to conceal, oppression is about at an end, though the Behais are secretive and obscurist still. The sect represents a revolt against the tyranny and fanaticism of the Koran and the laxity of Moslem practice, though allowing wine drinking and other leniencies. The Bab advocated also the removal of the veil by women, the disestablishment of the harem, and war against mendicancy. Doctrinely the Beha movement displaces Mohammed and the Koran, and regards God as a spiritual essence and not a person, while it yet compromises and conceals and now no longer wars against Shiahism.

As illustrated by this Babi movement, from the orthodox beliefs of the Shiahs there have been reactions, three of which among others have an influence in the present missionary situation in Persia; the mystical reaction of Sufiism which ran into pantheism and this modern Babism; the sceptical reaction, represented, for example, by Omar Khayam; and the stern revolt against the deification of Imams and holy men, which led to the mechanical views of the divine unity preached by the Wahabis. The dervishes grew profusely out of the Sufi movement, of whom Jelal-ud-din, the founder of the Maulavi Dervishes is the best spokesman:

Persia

"I was ere a name had been named upon earth,
Ere one trace yet existed of aught that had birth;
When the locks of the Loved One streamed forth for a sign,
And Being was none, save the Presence Divine.
Named and name were alike emanations from Me,
Ere aught that was I existed, or 'we.'

* * * * * * *

"The seventh heaven I traversed—the seventh heaven explored,
But in neither discerned I the court of the Lord!
I questioned the Pen and the Tablet of fate
But they whispered not where he pavilions his state.
My vision I strained; but my God-scanning eye
No trace that to Godhead belongs could descry;
My glance I bent inward; within my own breast;
Lo the vainly sought elsewhere, the Godhead confessed;
In the whirl of its transport my spirit was tossed,
Till each atom of separate being I lost."

Omar Khayam's note of weary scepticism is worth setting over against this:

"One moment in annihilation's waste,
One moment of the well of life to taste,
The stars are setting and the caravan
Starts for the dawn of nothing—oh make haste!

"Ah, fill the cup;—what boots it to repeat
How time is slipping underneath our feet;
Unborn to-morrow, and dead yesterday,
Why fret about them if to-day be sweet?

* * * * * * *

"That inverted bowl we call the sky.
Where under crawling coop'd we live and die,
Lift not thy hands to it for help—for it
Rolls impotently on as thou or I."

As for the Wahabis, whose movement prevailed rather in Arabia and India, their doctrine of God was ultra-Koranic, and their reaction was just an excessive and mechanical affirmation of Mohammed's theistic teachings, which there was danger

Missions and Politics

of confusing in the multiplicity of holy men.[1] No acknowledged Imam has aroused Persia for long generations, however, and the early views of the Deity have in general reasserted themselves, so that whatever can be said of the Mohammedan theology and its influence elsewhere, is applicable to Persia independent of these three movements of pantheism, scepticism and deism. Certain features of Shiahism, however, are peculiar, and have produced peculiar results which must be noted by themselves.

At the present time then, the general situation is just this: Persia is the stronghold of the Shiah sect whose doctrines possess its people with a strange fanaticism. Yet the Mohammedan religion is a distinct ecclesiastical organization, having no political power, and hedged in and curtailed as an influence by the present dynasty, which while holding the Shiah faith and asserting it as the State religion, still is and can but be in the place of a usurper of the rights of Ali's line. Religiously, Persia is isolated from Turkey which is Sunnite, and politically there is no commerce; for Islam can have but one head, and Muzaffr-i-din is as far from recognizing Abdul Hamid as that head, as the Sultan is from bowing to the Shah.

[1] Sell's *Faith of Islam*, Ed., 1880, chap. iii.

Persia

This situation suggests its own problems. I will not say that a Moslem unification is impossible. If seen to be clearly advantageous, self-interest would probably produce it as Shamil welded Sunnee and Shiah in the Caucasus a generation ago. But it is wholly improbable, and would have elements of disastrous weakness if ever attempted. The destinies of Sunnee and Shiah seem to lie apart, while Shiahism is rent and seamed with schism. Can, then, Persia stand alone and alone develop? Are the internal conditions of Church and State such as to promise stability? If not, what are the relations between Persia and Shiahism on one side, and non-Moslem States and religion on the other which will determine the future of the country. When we have answered these questions we shall be able perhaps to discern the general outlines of the divine history which is now making in Persia.

1. The condition of religion in Persia. Let us judge it first by its moral fruits. Sell points out that, "at first sight it would seem as if the doctrine of the Imamat might to some extent reconcile the thoughtful Shiah to the Christian doctrine of the Incarnation and Mediation of Jesus Christ, to His office as the perfect revealer of God's will, and as our Guide in life; but it is not so. The

Missions and Politics

mystic lore connected with Shiah doctrine has sapped the foundation of moral life and vigor. A system of religious reservation, too, is a fundamental part of the system in its mystical developments, whilst all Shiahs may lawfully practise 'takia' or religious compromise in their daily lives." The leader of the Babis gave his disciples a full dispensation to dissemble. "It thus becomes impossible to place dependence on what a Shiah may profess, as pious frauds are legalized by his system of religion. If he becomes a mystic, he looks upon the ceremonial and the moral law as restrictions imposed by an Almighty Power. The omission of the one is a sin, almost, if not quite as bad as a breach of the other. The advent of Mahdi is the good time when all such restrictions shall be removed, when the utmost freedom shall be allowed. Thus the moral sense, in many cases, becomes deadened to an extent, such as those who are not in daily contact with these people can hardly credit. The practice of 'takia,' religious compromise, and the legality of 'mutah' or temporary marriage have done much to demoralize the Shiah community."[1]

Osborn's words in *Islam under the Khalifs*

---

[1] Sell's *Faith of Islam*, Edition, 1880, pp. 83, 84.
Rodwell's *Koran*, London Ed., 1876, p. 451.

Persia

(p. 139) are scarcely too severe. "There can be no stronger testimony of the corrupting power, and the hard and hopeless bondage of the orthodox creed, than that men should escape from it into a system which established falsehood as the supreme law of conduct, and regarded the reduction of men to the level of swine as the goal of human existence."

This is stern judgment, but who that has seen the position of woman in a Mohammedan land can say that it is too stern? In social life Mohammedanism never conceived of a home. In Persian there are no distinct words for wife and home. The words for woman and house serve instead. The Prophet's example and teaching, the latter claiming to be the revelation of God, made it certain that Mohammedan life should forever lack all that for which in our Christian life the home stands. As to Mohammed's example, Marcus Dods' estimate of the man is but fair, "After Kadijah's influence was withdrawn, his relations with women were of a thoroughly discreditable kind.[1] His morality at this point was not that of a high-minded or spiritual man." As to his teaching, the Koran declares, "Of other women who seem good in

---

[1] Dods' *Mohammed, Buddha, Christ*, p. 24.

your eyes, marry but two or three or four" (Koran, Sura iv. 3). "Who control their desires, save with their wives or the slaves whom their right hands have won,—in that case verily they shall be blameless; . . . these shall dwell, laden with honors amid gardens" (Koran, Sura lxx. 29, 30, 35).[1] Thus Mohammed granted his followers in all times what in practical life amounts to unlimited polygamy, lust, divinely legalized, to suit the taste and wealth of all. The late Shah, a Persian army officer told me in Teheran, left in his harem when he died, 1,400 women, 104 of whom were recognized as legal wives, the rest as concubines and attendants. The present Shah said some years ago, that his father had fifty-six wives. Few Persians, of course, are able to support such establishments. Probably one-half are monogamists of necessity through poverty. But for the satisfaction of these, and with the effect of rendering true home life impossible for them, the Koran provides for divorce at will. "Ye may divorce your wives twice. Then if the husband divorce her a third time it is not lawful for him to take her again until she shall have married another husband; and if he also divorce her, then shall no blame

[1] Rodwell's *Koran*, London Ed., 1876, p. 60.

Persia

attach to them if they return to each other" (Koran, Sura ii. 229, 230). In accordance with these provisions men may take and discharge wives when they will. The words of the Koran regarding the return of the dower, or hire, as the Koran coarsely calls it, constitute practically no defence for the wife. She has no remedy, no resource. She must do what she can with her life. Under such practices and ideals it is not strange that one sees in Persia, not the attractive women, and the stalwart men of whom the books speak, but wrecked and weakly men and women, aged and shrivelled before their time. It is significant that the provisions regarding divorce contained in the Koran are in a Sura named "The Cow." That is woman's grade. "An inferior, dependent creature," says Sir Wm. Muir, "destined only for the service of her master. . . . Who possessed," adds Muir, "more freedom and exercised a healthier and more legitimate influence under the pagan institutions of Arabia before the time of Mohammed, than under the influence of Islam."

Nowhere has Islam done its deadly work in this regard more fearfully than in Persia. In a report on Persia in 1873, Polak, who was a physician, named as the first main cause of the decline of the population, "the unfavorable position of women, including the facility of divorce, early marriage and premature age." I understood after seeing Persia, the reason for one Persian woman's words to Mrs. Hawkes of Hamadan: "Your Prophet did well for your women. Ours did not. I shall have words with our Prophet when I see him in the next world," and how another could cry out of her wretchedness, "When the gates of hell are opened, the Mussulman men will go in first."[1]

It has been claimed for Islam that its provisions regarding marriage and divorce have abolished the vice of prostitution, and made Moslem lands in this respect cleaner than Christian lands. It might be replied that the authorized Moslem practices regarding women render this a superfluous and unnecessary vice; but it may be worth while to accept the challenge and measure Persian Mohammedanism by it. Prostitution has not been abolished. It flourishes under ecclesiastical sanction in many čities, but notably in Meshed. Meshed is the holiest city of Persia, the burial place of the preëminently holy Imam Reza, the son of Imam Musa, and the eighth of

[1] Wilson's *Persian Life and Customs*, N. Y. Ed., 1895, p. 226.

Persia

the twelve Imams. To this shrine 100,000 pilgrims annually toil from all parts of Persia. "In recognition of the long journeys which they have made," says Curzon,[1] "of the hardships which they have sustained, and of the distance by which they are severed from family and home, they are permitted, with the connivance of the ecclesiastical law and its officers, to contract temporary marriages during their sojourn in the city. There is a large permanent population of wives (in connection with the shrine) for this purpose. . . . In other words, a gigantic system of prostitution under the sanction of the Church prevails in Meshed." The Mollahs themselves draw up the temporary contracts, "There is probably not a more immoral city in Asia." Shiah Mohammedanism has not only not abolished this awful evil, it lends to it its Mollahs and its mosques. Of yet viler vices which it has fostered, I will not venture to speak; or of the evidence that intemperance, opium eating, falsehood, cruelty to children, are other fruits of Islam in Persia, or, if they are not its fruits, have at least grown up substantially unchecked by it, and uncondemned by the Mollahs. Regarding these, Curzon claims that Conolly was well

---

[1] Curzon's *Persia*, London Ed., 1892, Vol. I., p. 165.

within the mark when he wrote of the priests of one of Shiahism's most holy shrines, "The greater number of these are rogues, who only take thought of how to make the most of the pilgrims who visit the shrine. From the high priest to the seller of bread, all have the same end; and not content with the strangers' money, those in office about the saint appropriate to themselves the very dues for keeping the temple in order."

2. In addition to utter failure in moral and social life, Islam has wrought out its own condemnation in politics. This condemnation has been due, and in the present history of Persia can still be traced to the Moslem idea of God, and the Moslem doctrine of the Koran. There is much that is stimulating and true in the conception of God presented by Mohammed. "God!" cried he, "There is no God but He—the living, the self-subsisting; neither slumber seizes Him, nor sleep; all that is in the heavens and in the earth is His. Who is he that can intercede with Him but by His own permission? He knoweth what is present with His creatures, and what is yet before them; yet naught of His knowledge do they comprehend, save what He willest. His throne reacheth over the heavens and the earth, and the

upholding of both burdeneth Him not. And He is the High, the Great." There is a tonic in such teaching beside which the miasmic pantheism of India is as mire. And to this God, the High, the Great, Mohammed preached sole submission. This was Islam. "Islam means" as Thomas Carlyle says in *Heroes and Hero Worship*, (Chap. ii.) "that we must submit to God, that our whole strength lies in resigned submission to Him, whatsoever He do to us. . . . It has ever been held," Carlyle adds, "the highest wisdom for a man, not merely to submit to necessity—necessity will make him submit—but to know and believe well that the stern thing which necessity had ordered was the wisest, the best, the thing wanted there; to cease his frantic pretension of scanning this great God's world in his small fraction of a brain; to know that it had verily, though deep beyond his soundings, a just law; that the sum of it was good; that his part was to conform to the law of the whole and in devout silence follow that; not questioning it, obeying it as unquestionable. This is the soul of Islam; it is properly the soul of Christianity,"—submission. And even so good a Christian as Bishop Butler says, "Submission is the whole of religion." I trust not of ours, though it be of

Missions and Politics

Mohammed's and Mohammed's followers'. This is its weakness as well as its strength. It fills men with the fierce fanaticism of God's servants. It gives them none of the love and gentleness of God's sons. "I have called you slaves," says Mohammed. "I have called you friends," said Christ.

Islam has not provided for fellowship with God. He spoke by Mohammed. The Koran is the last sound of His voice human ears have heard. Of a living God speaking to the soul and dwelling there as the light of our light and the life of our life, Islam does not dream. God the Eternal One, begetting not, not begotten, sits on His throne and watches His mighty machinery roll out the unchangeable, predestined result. He speaks not, neither does He hear. The deaf and dumb God drives the engines of fate. "Inshallah," "Kismet," are the words of Islam, and "He loves," "He cares," "He hears," are alien to its creed.

Such a deism is the death of progress. Its God "sterile in His inaccessible height, neither loving nor enjoying aught save His own and self-measured decree, without son, companion or councillor, is no less barren for Himself than for His creatures, and His own barrenness and lone

Persia

egoism in Himself is the cause and rule of His indifferent and unregarding despotism around." In its essence, therefore, as Palgrave declares, Islam must be stationary. It "was formed thus to remain. Sterile like its God, lifeless like its first Principle, and supreme Original in all that constitutes true life—(for life is love, participation and progress, and of these the Koranic Deity has none)—it justly repudiates all change, all advance, all development."[1]

And not only is there no germ or justification of life and progress in the Mohammedan idea of God, but the Prophet wholly blocked the possibility of these by stereotyping forever the forms and spirit of his religion in the Koran. To temporary expedients and customs the Koran gave permanent form and sanction. It stultifies itself and its religion by erecting thus into permanent institutions the semi-savage conceptions and adjustments of the seventh century in Arabia. It cannot alter. The mould has set:

> "So while the world rolls on from change to change,
> And realms of thought expand,
> The letter stands without expanse or range
> Stiff as a dead man's hand."

Nowhere have these petrifying, stagnating influences of Islam borne more evident fruit than in

[1] Palgrave's *Arabia*, Vol. I., pp. 369, 372.

Missions and Politics

Persia. For twelve centuries the land has been Moslem. During those centuries some notable characters have arisen; in science, Avicenna, in medicine, Nasr-i-din, in astronomy; in poetry, Firdousi, Saadi, Hafiz; in war and government, Shah Abbas the Great. But Islam is to be credited with none of these. It was the outburst of the strong old Persian character. We may say of it what Renan said of the flourishing of science and philosophy on Mussulman soil during the first half of the Middle Ages, "It was not by reason of Islam. It was in spite of Islam." It has happened in Persia as Fairbairn declares has happened elsewhere, "The Koran has frozen Mohammedan thought. To obey it has been to abandon progress."

Like a wreck, a ruin, a memory of far-distant greatness, the Persian Nation lies in evidence of the paralysis of Islam. There are no schools, save here and there chattering groups around a village priest, or worse than mediæval groups around a mesjid and a mujtahid. The few schools of the government in Tabriz, and Teheran are chiefly opportunities for officials to eat up public revenues. Charitable institutions are practically unknown. Prisons are mere places of torture until the demanded money fine is paid. Houses of permanent detention or reformation

Persia

for evil doers do not exist. Death or payment or torture are the ends of the law. The courts half civil, half ecclesiastical, are irregular, with no written codes, no jury system, no pleading, no testimony, save the eloquence and evidence of bribes. The sects of Shiahism riot when they please in internecine strife, plunder and murder. The attempts to imitate some of the external ways of civilization have ended in bathos. The postal system is a despair, the couriers lounging idly along the road, taking often a week to go 200 miles, while postmasters take letters from the mail when they please and are the tools of government. The telegraph system is yet more of a farce. Whole sentences were omitted from our messages. The posts lie on the ground with the wires under the feet of the caravans. Telegrams are often as long on the road as letters, and the senders frequently arrive before their messages. The roads are mere trails. One or two were built once but they are falling into ruin. The post houses and caravansaries are tumbling down. Bridges are no concern of the government, and are cared for only by those who absolutely need them or would make heavenly merit. The army, with wages of two cents a day and pay a year in arrears, tattered and sickly, is too sad a sight to

Missions and Politics

be ludicrous. Villages are owned by proprietors usually living in some distant city, and bleeding them through ravenous collectors. All enterprise is throttled by taxation. The land lies smitten and in despair. Offices are bought and sold, and each purchaser squeezes at once every dollar possible out of those placed in his power, to reimburse himself for his bribes, and to prepare for his removal, which may come at any hour. The village homes are as poor as well can be, and the villager fears prosperity as the sure promise that fresh tax levies will pinch him more than before.[1] Saddest of all is the decadence of religious perception, the want of moral stamina, the prevalence of deceit, falsehood, rottenness of life, of all of which there is no stronger evidence than the throngs of dervishes, the holy men of Islam, who wander up and down the land, loathsome beyond words.

The decadence of Persia began long ago, but Islam has only accelerated its pace, having done nothing to cleanse or to save. A son of Fath Ali Shah, the great-grandfather of the present Shah, who though an old and bent man, was about to start on a pilgrimage to Mecca, told me that the land had gone down, down, down, each year. I asked

---

[1] Curzon s *Persia*, Vol. I., chaps. xiv., xv.

Persia

two of the most judicious natives in Oroomiah, whether the condition was hopeless. "Yes," they said, "the country is going steadily from worse to worse. Nothing can save Persia till Islam is broken." Another remedy is the longing of thousands of Persians. A young nobleman on the Kum road, expressed it to us when he said, "There must be a protectorate or a division soon. There is no hope save in Russia or England."

"In vain did Mohammed," said Professor Smyth in his Oxford *Lectures on Modern History*, "destroy the idols of his countrymen and sublimate their faith to the worship of the one true God," —and all his words apply with equal truth to Persia—"in vain did he inculcate compassion to the distressed, alms to the needy, protection and tenderness to the widow and the orphan. He neither abolished nor discountenanced polygamy, and the professors of his faith have been thus left the domestic tyrants of one-half of their own race. He taught predestination, and they have thus become by their crude application of his doctrine, the victims of every natural disease and calamity. He practised intolerance, and they are thus made the enemies of the civilized world. He permitted the union of the royal and sacerdotal offices, and he made the book of his religion and his legislation the same. All alteration therefore, among the Mohammedans must have been thought impiety. Last in the scale of thinking beings, they have exhibited families without society, subjects without freedom, governments without security and nations without improvement."

The living God to whom all lies are abhorrent has wrought out the demonstration of Mohammedanism's failure and curse beyond a chance of misunderstanding. But what is to become of the wreck? There are two forces shaping the future even now. One is political. Persia is one of that group of intermediate states between the Russian Power and the British Empire in India, which are being crushed as the pack ice is crushed between approaching icebergs. The Russian eagles hang about Ararat and watch from the North bank of the Aras river over the province of Azerbijan, in the Northwest. The Caspian Sea is wholly in Russia's control on the North, and Russia's railroad and encampments lie along the Northeast, beyond the province of Khorasan. On the other hand, British boats control the Tigris, and therefore the Southwest of Persia. Bushire is within call of India, and

Persia

British war ships are ever lying there. The gulf coast of Persia is regarded in India as semi-British and Muscat, which is semi-British also, is within hail across the Persian Gulf, while around the Southeastern corner of Persia the British sentinels wait. "It should not be forgotten," says the *Times* of India, "that the real frontier of the Indian Empire is not the scene of the recent conflicts with the Afridi and Waziri tribes, but that it stretches virtually from the mouth of the Shat-el-Arab, at the head of the Persian Gulf, along the Southern borders of Afghanistan and Thibet to Burmah and Yunnan." And as on the East, Russia creeps down from Bokhara, Great Britain creeps up from Peshawur. If within the land the British Minister was the Shah until the son could be brought to sit on the throne which his father's assassination had made vacant, the Russian Minister has played Shah since when it suited him. Whose will Persia be? Great Britain does not want it. The trade would not pay for the cost and trouble of government. That is the final test. Russia does not want Persia yet. There is too much else in hand. That Russia is unprepared was clearly shown by her failure to support the Greek priests who in 1897 stampeded the Nestorians with hope of Russia's protection, and then for a time, at least, abandoned them to worse oppression when the Russian civil authorities declined to fulfill the promises of their ecclesiastics. Great Britain and Russia are not yet where they could jointly occupy or hold protectorate over a land. But if that day should come, the Eastern Question would be solved. The whole heart of that question is the jealousy of these two Powers. Then the Turk would leave Europe, and Persia would be cleansed and set upon her feet. Meanwhile politically the game will be a balance between these two in Persia with the odds ever in Russia's favor, and a fair pretext for interference always at hand in the relations of the Nestorians to the Greek Church.

The other force that is at work in Persia is Missions. It is an intruder. The presence of Missions in a Moslem land is inconsistent with the character of Islam, which requires that all non-Moslems shall accept the Koran, pay tribute, or be put to the sword, and whose precise instructions, never revoked, are "Fight thou against them (Jews and Christians) until they pay tribute by right of subjection, and they be reduced low," (Koran, Sura ix. 30). To send missionaries to Islam if it be true to itself, therefore, is to thrust men into the lion's den. It is for this

Persia

reason that Islam has been so shunned as a Mission field. It had dealt with Christianity and claimed to be its successor and superior, and whoever would not acknowledge this it proposed to humiliate, or to put to death. Accordingly, among the great heroes of missionary history men rank Francis of Assisi and Raymond Lull,[1] the former because in 1219, though there was a price on every Christian's head, he marched in his mendicant's grey robe and cord of self-denial, chanting the twenty-third Psalm, into the very midst of the Saracen hosts, which were then besieged in Damietta by an army of crusading Franks; and the latter, because a century later, after missionary labors never surpassed, he was stoned to death by Moslems, to whose evangelization he had devoted his life, true in death as in all living service to the motto from his own great book, "He who loves not, lives not; and he who lives by the Life cannot die." These were great heroisms and rare; in missionaries to the Mohammedans our own century has been richer far.

Henry Martyn was the first of this band in Persia. Coming from India, he passed through on his way to Tocat, where in compliance with

[1] Smith's *Short History of Christian Missions*, pp. 101-108.

Missions and Politics

his own earlier prayer, he burned out for God. In 1811 he wished to present his translation of the New Testament and Psalms to the king. The greeting he received in this attempt is worth recalling: "June 12th," he wrote, "I attended the vizier's levee when there was a most intemperate and clamorous controversy kept up for an hour or two, eight or ten on one side and I on the other. . . . The vizier, who set us going at first, joined in it latterly, and said, 'You had better say God is God and Mohammed is the prophet of God.' I said, 'God is God,' but added instead of 'Mohammed is the prophet of God,' 'and Jesus is the Son of God.' They had no sooner heard this, which I had avoided bringing forward until then, than they all exclaimed in contempt and anger, 'He is neither born nor begets,' and rose as if they would have torn me in pieces. One of them said, 'What will you say when your tongue is burned out for this blasphemy?' One of them felt for me a little and tried to soften the severity of this speech. My book, which I had brought, expecting to present it to the king, lay before Mirza Shufi. As they all rose up after him to go, some to the king and some away, I was afraid they would trample upon the book, so I went among them to

Persia

take it up and wrapped it in a towel before them, while they looked at it and me with supreme contempt. Thus I walked away alone to pass the rest of the day in heat and dirt. What have I done, thought I, to merit all this scorn? Nothing, thought I, but bearing testimony to Jesus. I thought over these things in prayer, and found that peace which Christ hath promised to His disciples."[1]

The spirit which Henry Martyn encountered eighty-one years ago is the spirit of Persian Moslems still. The attempt to carry on an open and continued propaganda among them would lead to the expulsion of the missionaries from the country, if indeed it did not lead to riot, incendiarism and murder. Principal Grant of Queen's University, Canada, innocently suggests in his little book on *The Religions of the World* (p. 40), that "we can approach them (the Moslems) in the spirit of brotherhood, as men having a common heritage. We can show to all (of them) who are reasonable and who appreciate the methods and principles of modern criticism, that there is the fullest proof for the accuracy of our Scriptures—better proof, indeed, than for any other ancient documents." We can

[1] Smith's *Henry Martyn*, pp. 466, 467.

indeed, and when Persia opens to the study of comparative religion and of modern literary criticism it will be fatal to Mohammedanism, but as yet the number of Persians "who are reasonable and who appreciate the principles and methods of modern criticism" is so small as to be undiscoverable, while the host who cry out against the infidels, and who respond to the fanatical incitements of the ecclesiastics is very great, so great as to have made many missionaries tremble, and to have won for not a few native Christians the crown of martyrdom.

How is it then, it may be asked, that since 1835 the missionaries have been allowed to live and work so freely in the country? The answer is twofold.

1 They have been allowed to stay and work because their base of work was among non-Moslem people. There were in Persia before the Kurdish outrages, about 20,000 Jews, 45,000 Armenians and 25,000 Nestorians. Since the massacres in Turkey, the numbers of Armenians and Nestorians have been greatly increased by the flocks of refugees who have come over into Persia. These non-Moslem communities, which are wholly subject and suffer many grievous disabilities, especially the Jews, have a recognized stand-

Persia

ing, and have been secured in the practice of their own religions. Missionary work among them has been both allowed and encouraged by the government, and settling among them and secure in his relationship to them, the missionary has been free to do unlimited work among the Moslems if he does it prudently and tactfully, and with as much conciliation as the conflict of his truth with Moslem error will allow.

Perhaps it was with some such purpose that the Providence of God settled these small bodies in Persia. The Christianity of Gregorian and Nestorian was a reproach. It fortified rather than weakened Moslem conviction as to the superiority of Islam. The Mussulman has treated them with contempt and looked down on their ancient Churches with disdain; but when we think of the old Code of Omar and its exactions that the graves of Christians should be level with the ground, the mark of the devil should be on the lintel of their doors, that all freedom and aspiration should be proscribed to them and their worship be degraded, and their homes, their wives and their honor humbled; and when we remember that they have under the abuse of centuries maintained at least their existence and the Christian name; and realize that without the

Missions and Politics

opportunity they provide we should probably be without access to Islam in Persia, we temper our judgment, though we recognize their degradation and need.[1]

As to the future of the non-Moslem peoples under the Shah, hope grows dim. From 1870 to 1890 their condition seemed to improve steadily, as the Shah increased his power and authority over the ecclesiastics and strengthened the central government. Since 1890, however, the ecclesiastics have been regaining their lost ground, and the central Government has been disintegrating, and disorder and fear now prevail. And for these and their hard lot in general, the Armenians and Nestorians, not unnaturally hold responsible the so-called Christian Nations, and consequently their representatives, the missionaries. The education of these people under systems which combine State and Church prevents their discriminating in our case between the pagan acts of our Governments and the Christian professions of our religion. And this is quite intelligible to us also, when we remember the way Western Nations have laid themselves open in this matter. To gain political power they used the pretexts of desire to defend fellow Christians, and when such

[1] Muir's *Caliphate*, London Ed., 1892, p. 147.

Persia

defence imperilled political power disavowed all such responsibility. That this was true especially in Turkey, does not prevent the Persian Christians from feeling the mockery and deception of it.

Among these non-Moslem peoples, noble fruits of missionary effort have been gathered; but looking far forward, their chief significance is found in their relation and the relation of the work among them, to the coming conflict with Islam.

2 The other reason for the non-molestation of the Missions is found in the high character and ability of the missionaries, and the influence they have gained in the country. General Wagner, an Austrian officer, the drill master of the Persian army, who has been for nearly twenty years in Persia, and who came to Teheran with the present Shah, said to me, "Tell the Church in America that I have seen the missionaries, and have studied their work in Oroomiah, Salmas, Tabriz and Teheran. I know about it. It is not a human work. It is an angel work. They are all angels." The old general's confidence in the missionaries was greater than his knowledge of English. And when a missionary present tried to turn the edge of his remark, and happened to use the word heaven, "Yes," said General Wagner,

Missions and Politics

catching the new word, "it is a heaven work—a heaven work." The acting Dutch minister who was present, added, "All the rest of us are here for money. The missionaries are here to do good. It is the noblest, the only good work in Persia."

The day before we left Teheran, Sir Mortimer Durand, the British Minister, and one of the ablest British diplomatists in Asia, came up at the close of a service held for Europeans, and said that he had not had opportunity before to say as strongly as he wished, and perhaps could not say strongly enough, how much the Europeans in Persia, and he personally, were indebted to the missionaries and to the American Church for sending them; how much good they did, how great their influence was in the land.

This view of the leading foreigners could be supported by the words of governors and princes who agreed in the testimony of Prince Azad-i-dowleh, governor of Hamadan, a venerable man, who, during our last call upon him, laid his hand with real confidence upon the arm of one of the missionaries, and said, "These gentlemen and I are warm friends, brothers." Even among the Shiah mollahs the missionaries have friends who

Persia

respect them, and might protect them. And in general, Shiah Mohammedans in Persia seem more open than the Sunnees of Turkey, while yet they are usually esteemed more fanatical and bigoted, and while those doubtless are right who see only evil and the promise of evil in the ecclesiastics. That there should be any friendliness and accessibility is quite illogical, to be sure, and it shows that the hold of Islam has weakened.

As indeed it has. It is true that the number of open converts from Mohammedanism is small, that those who openly confess Christ are persecuted and sometimes put to death. Mirza Ibrahim was thus killed only five years ago. But the shackles of their faith hang lightly on thousands of Mussulmans. I have seen half a dozen mollahs come to a Christian service, and listen with great respect and interest. And the influence of a pure and living faith has reached far and wide through Persia. "Yes," said a peasant who ran along the road to talk with us in a remote part of the land, "I know your religion. It is a good religion." Some day Persia will come to it.

The late Dr. Shedd of Oroomiah maintained that Persia is the weak point of Mohammedanism for the reasons that (a) the Persians being branded as heretics by the Sunnees, turn rather to Christians for aid and sympathy than to the rival sect, and are more accessible than any other Moslems to the Christian missionary, (b) that the Persians as a people are more liberal and tolerant than any other Moslem nation, (c) that in Persia Mohammedanism is divided against itself more than in any other land, new heretical sects constantly arising which are more hostile to the other sects of Islam than they are to Christianity, and (d) that Mohammedanism has failed to help and bless the people. The people are coming to see its fruits and also the fruits of Christianity. Other missionaries believe that Mohammedanism has lost its hold on multitudes of the people, that they are simply amused at it, that if Islam can be attacked anywhere it is in Persia. One of the most experienced and successful native workers among the Moslems, expressed the excessive belief that thousands of Mohammedans would accept Christianity if there were religious liberty.

To return then at the close to the thought with which I introduced this lecture, we are looking now on a State whose old forces are decadent and corrupt. Its old history has run to a close.

Persia

There is no life or progress in the Persian State. There is no life or progress, though vast latent fanaticism, in the Persian religion. New forces must make the new history. The new forces are creeping in. Two great Nations stand on either side. The advent of either means order. The advent of one means progress. I believe the advent of the other means progress also, only with slower step. And Christianity has already entered. It has wrought quietly, awaiting the day when the external chains of Islam will be taken off, and men will be free to move; but it has wrought mightily. The old forces waning; the waxing of the new. We see all this. But we see more, one certain ground of faith; for the doom of Islam as a dominant tyranny cannot be far distant now in Persia. The State that once ruled the world, that once was the world, is shattered, aged and doddering. Shiahism which broke off from orthodox Mohammedanism, and contributed for a while to the strengthening of Persia as a separate State, has also weakened, sapped of life and genuine power, however fervent its fanaticism and however strong its hold may still be on the ecclesiastic and the poor. "The dead man's hand," as Lord Houghton

Missions and Politics

called it, has been long upon the land, but the time of its lifting will come, because,

> " As the lifeblood fills the growing form,
>   The Spirit Christ has shed,
> Flows through the ripening ages fresh and warm
>   More felt than heard or read.
>
> " And, therefore, tho ancestral sympathies
>   And closest ties of race
> May guard Mohammed's precepts and decrees
>   Through many a tract of space,
>
> " Yet in the end the tight drawn line must break,
>   The sapless tree must fall,
> Nor let the form one time did well to take,
>   Be tyrant over all."

LECTURE II

Southern Asia

"*We work on the refuse of worked-out cities and exhausted civilizations, among the bones of the dead.*"

Pagett laughed. "That's an epigrammatic way of putting it, Orde."

"Is it? Let's see," said the Deputy Commissioner of Amara, striding into the sunshine toward a half-naked gardener potting roses. He took the man's hoe, and went to a rain-scarped bank at the bottom of the garden.

"Come here, Pagett," he said, and cut at the sun-baked soil. After three strokes, there rolled from under the blade of the hoe, the half of a clanking skeleton that settled at Pagett's feet in an unseemly jumble of bones. The M. P. drew back.

"Our houses are built on cemeteries," said Orde. "There are scores of thousands of graves within ten miles."

Pagett was contemplating the skull with the awed fascination of a man who has but little to do with the dead.

"India's a very curious place," said he, after a pause.

RUDYARD KIPLING, *The Enlightenments of Pagett, M. P.*

LECTURE II

SOUTHERN ASIA

Turkey

AFTER five busy months in Persia, we left Hamadan in the depth of winter for the long ride over "The Corpse Road" to Bagdad, and having been already unduly delayed, we crossed Southern Asia as speedily as was convenient in order to reach China in the early Spring. This led us through Turkey, Arabia, India, Burmah and the Straits. In this lecture accordingly, I would speak of the present situation and of the present play of political and religious forces in the three peninsulas which stand in something more than a fanciful relationship to Spain, Italy and Greece, their counterparts in Europe.

It was with a feeling of deep awe that we drew near the edge of the Persian plateau, and waited for the moment when from the last mountains we could look down on the valleys which would lead us out to the wide plains where forty centuries ago Abraham fed his flocks, and the children of Abraham's son Isaac

Missions and Politics

once hung their harps upon the willows, but where the children of Abraham's son Ishmael now roam in the solitudes. The driving snow, however, hid the valleys from view. But the land falls sheer away from the last Westward brow of the Zagros range, and in five hours we were free of winter and storm, and riding under the clear sun, and in three days in the midst of palm and orange trees, until at last across a broad plain, whose horizon line seemed ever to recede, cracked and seamed by the water and the sun, and broken only by the ruins of ancient water trenches or by soft marshes, we saw the great wealth of deep green palm fronds overtopped by the glittering domes and minarets which told us that the weary journey from old Ecbatana to the City of the Caliphs was done.

Bagdad is the seat of government of the extreme Southeastern provinces, the most remote section of the Turkish Empire. They were part of the first territorial conquests of Islam. In 634 Khalid had taken Damascus. Two years later the Arab armies drove Heraclius out of Syria, and defeated the Persians at Kadesia. Jerusalem fell the following year. By the end of the seventh century the Saracens had reached the Oxus in Asia, having conquered Persia, Bokhara

Southern Asia

and Turkestan, and Spain and lower Gaul had fallen before them on the West where Akba spurring his horse into the sea had cried, "Great God, if my course were not stopped by the sea, I would still go on to the unknown kingdoms of the West, preaching the unity of Thy Holy Name, and putting to the sword the rebellious nations which refuse to call upon Thee."[1] To this victorious march in the West, Charles Martel set a limit in 732, and three centuries later the Arabs were driven out of Italy. Their Western losses were repaired, however, by Eastern conquests under the Turks, who had supplanted the Arabs and who reached Jerusalem in 1076; while in the thirteenth century the Seljukian Turks were succeeded by the Ottomans who took Constantinople in 1453, and set up the empire which has been the puzzle and the curse of European politics ever since. In these four centuries, however, the Turkish power in Europe has slowly crumbled away. Bosnia, Herzegovina, Illyricum, Greece, Transylvania, Moldavia, Besarabia, Podalia and the Euxine possessions have been stripped off, and the only apparently sure territory left is the Asia Minor provinces, while Russia hangs ominously over these.

[1] Bosworth Smith's *Mohammed and Mohammedanism*, pp. 30, 31.

Missions and Politics

I have neither time nor heart to discuss at any length the questions of European politics that concern the Ottoman Empire, but desire only to call attention to several points forced on the traveller through Southeastern Turkey in Asia.

1. The Turkish government is evil and corrupt, and ought to be brought to an end. The most earnest apologist for Mohammedanism and Mohammedan institutions, Mr. Bosworth Smith admits "The system of government, never an enlightened one, has at all events since the so-called reforms of the Sultan Mahmoud been rotten at the core. Stambul has become an asylum for the rascality of West and East alike; the finest peasantry in the world, the inhabitants of Asia Minor, are dying by starvation, partly, no doubt, owing to bad harvests, but still more owing to the neglect of the most ordinary precautions and duties of government. Roads unmade, bridges broken down, mines unworked, unprincipled and exorbitant provincial Pashas, wastefulness and disorder and excessive centralization,—such is the picture which travellers give us of these fair regions of the earth, and unfortunately we know it to be a true picture."[1] This was written twenty years ago. The condition is worse to-day. Men

[1] Smith's *Mohammed and Mohammedanism*, p. 179.

avoid prosperity and all evidence of thrift because the robbery and squeezing they invite are worse. than poverty and need. Unjust taxation, corrupt and merciless collections, farming of revenues, unlicensed official rottenness, are mild charges compared with what might be made. Rather than describe it, I prefer to quote the temperate words of Professor Freeman; "The Turk came in as an alien and barbarian encamped on the soil of Europe. At the end of 500 years, he remains an alien and barbarian encamped on soil which he has no more made his own than it was when he first took Kallipolis. His rule during all that time has been the rule of strangers over enslaved nations in their own land. It has been the rule of cruelty, faithlessness and brutal lust; it has not been government, but organized brigandage. His rule cannot be reformed. While all other nations get better and better, the Turk gets worse and worse. And when the chief powers of Europe join in demanding that he should make even the smallest reform, he impudently refuses to make any. If there was anything to be said for him before the late Conference, there is nothing to be said for him now. For an evil which cannot be reformed, there is one remedy only, to get rid of it. Justice, reason, humanity demand that the rule of the Turk in Europe should be got rid of, and the time for getting rid of it has now come."[1] I would only add to Freeman's words, that subsequent history has but served to show more plainly, to use Gladstone's phrase, the "damning disgrace" of leaving the door open for further Turkish outrage and iniquity; and that what is true of the corruption and injustice of European Turkey, is more true of those remote sections where the Turk has his own way undisturbed.

2. Secondly, if the Turkish government is hard upon the Arab and the Turk, it is yet harder upon the Christian. Christian tribes fought side by side with the Arab forces in the Persian wars, but the stern laws of Islam soon drew them into the great mortar wherein men were pounded into Islam, slavery, or eternity. Ever since, the lot of a Christian on Turkish soil, where the State and the Church are one, and the law of Islam is the law of the civil power, has been anomalous and it has been agony. For "the Mohammedan law," as the best of modern authorities has shown,[2] "(suspended to-day, but not repealed, being regarded as of divine appointment) prohibits peaceful relations with Mohammedans.

---
[1] Freeman's *The Turk in Europe.*
[2] Dwight's *Status of American Missionaries in Turkey.*

Southern Asia

Such relations would produce intermingling of interests, carefully warded off by the dispositions of the founder of the religion. It allows the Sovereign caliph to spare, if he choose, the lives of those in his dominions who refuse to accept the Moslem faith on condition of their paying a special tribute or head tax. But it provides that the collection of this tax be made harshly in order to remind the unbeliever of his abject condition as owing even his life to favor. It leaves the caliph free to grant peace to non-Mohammedan nations, but it requires him to break his treaties of peace as soon as good policy permits resumption of the war, rendered obligatory by the refusal of such nations to accept Islam. It permits him to grant safety to non-Mohammedan foreigners whom he may admit to his dominions, but it categorically declares that when such an alien has dwelt a year in Moslem territory, he must either become a Mussulman, become a Zimme (subject who pays head tax) or leave the country." That these laws are suspended does not alter the fact that they are unchanged and unchangeable as the laws of God, and have been so recognized by European ambassadors in Constantinople, who have accepted instead of their abrogation, an assurance that they will be held in abeyance. Only, wher-

Missions and Politics

ever and to the extent that their principles can be enforced, there they are enforced. Witness the murdered men, the outraged women, the orphan children, the pillaged homes of Armenia, Bulgaria, Lebanon, Damascus, Kurdistan and Chios, in the sickening massacres which have marked the alternate decades of the century.[1]

3. The Turkish Government has been held together by the so-called Christian Governments of Europe, who have professed to be acting constantly in the interests of the Christian subjects of the Sultan. In 1829, by the Treaty of Adrianople at the close of a war with Russia, Turkey promised to reform her treatment of Christians, and was obliged to acknowledge Russia's right to interfere in their behalf. In 1878, just before the famous Treaty of Berlin, an Anglo-Turkish convention was made with these words in the First Article, "His Imperial Majesty, the Sultan, promises to England to introduce necessary reforms to be agreed upon later between the two Powers, into the government and for the protection of the Christian and other subjects of the Porte in these territories (i. e. Armenia), and in order to enable England to make necessary provision for executing her engagement (the

[1] British *Blue Books*, Turkey, Nos. 1 and 2, 1896.

keeping of Russia out of Armenia) His Imperial Majesty, the Sultan, further consents to assign the Island of Cyprus to be occupied and administered by England." The Treaty of Berlin adopted the same year, declared in the Sixty-first Article, "The Sublime Porte undertakes to carry out without further delay, the improvements and reforms demanded by local requirements in the provinces inhabited by the Armenians, and to guarantee their security against the Circassians and Kurds. It will periodically make known the steps taken to this effect to the Powers, who will superintend their application." In these ways the European Nations and Great Britain, preëminently, entered into partnership with Turkey, and so supported, Turkey has been able to do and has done in the way of outrage and massacres what could not otherwise have been done. And to-day, her subjects, Moslem and Christian alike, Arab as well as Armenian in Mesopotamia, are suffering from an accentuation of the very evils of oppression and rotten government from which the Christian nations had engaged to deliver the Christians. And why? Because of jealousy and the interests of trade, Great Britain refusing to let Constantinople go to Russia because it would imperil her hold on Egypt and

Missions and Politics

the route to India and the East by Suez and the Red Sea. Treaty conventions and the lives of Christians were of no account in comparison with the Suez Canal. And yet many Englishmen in Persia or Turkey, even British consuls, candidly admit that Russia could be given Constantinople, as she will surely have it in time, without fear. This would bring to an end the Turk in Europe. To do that in some way, Professor Freeman declared was Great Britain's duty. "By waging a war on behalf of the Turk, by signing a treaty which left the nations of Southeastern Europe (and Asia Minor) at the mercy of the Turk, by propping up the wicked power of the Turk in many ways, we have done a great wrong to the nations which are under his yoke; and that wrong which we have ourselves done, it is our duty to undo." But undone as to Europe, the Turk would be left in Asia to rule from the Mediterranean to Persia, and from the Euxine to the Persian Gulf. And his government there, stronger far than the government of Persia, is bad, thoroughly bad. It keeps the Arab tribes from tribal wars, but it plunders them of their flocks and their crops, and spreads a trail of desolation over the whole land. Wherever Islam has gone it has either found a desert or made one.[1]

4. Dawn is still far distant in Eastern Turkey. A generation ago Mr. Palgrave thought the elements of permanency were coming into view when the Circassians, driven before Muscovite power, crossed the Turkish frontier and "coalescing with Kurds, Turkomans and Arabs," settled down on the uplands of Armenia and began there, as he believed, the formation of the nucleus of a new and vigorous and united Mohammedan nation. Mr. Bosworth Smith seized upon Mr. Palgrave's opinion and looked zealously forward to the growth of the new nation, the healing of the breach between Sunnee and Shiah, even as in the days of Shamil, a regeneration of Islam which would lift it with the old hot Arab breath to stay the conquering march of the Russian Colossus.[2] The spread of Islam was to him a blessing and a joy compared with the growing dominion of the Czar. The new nation has not come, and whoso looks for a united Mohammedanism, forged into a stable, advancing nation, will look long and will look in vain. The races and religion of Turkey in Asia have their ele-

[1] Greene's *The Armenian Crisis in Turkey*, chaps. v., viii.
Ramsay's *Impressions of Turkey*, chaps. vi., vii.
[2] Smith's *Mohammed and Mohammedanism*, pp. 270, 271.

ments of strength, but they have no elements of progress; and though the real faith of Islam is capable of being fanned into fanaticism and war again and again, its hold on conscience has weakened, and its power has decayed forever.

5. Fifthly, it must be confessed that the forces of Christian faith among the Christian subjects of Turkey and of Christian Missions have as yet played no great part in the development of history in Southeastern Turkey. It has been a field little tilled by missionaries. For some years the C. M. S.[1] has maintained a feeble station at Bagdad, and far to the North, American missionaries have worked from Mardin and Mosul. Mosul has been abandoned, however, and Mardin is greatly limited in its work. Looking out over the broad plains which stretch from the Tigris to the Euphrates and beyond, with their hundreds of Bedouin tribes, or passing through the crowded bazaars of Bagdad and Busra with their memories of their Arab founders in the days of Islam's youth, and considering how feeble is the effort which the Church is making for the evangelization of these people, one is deeply impressed with the truth that God has other forces by which He works toward His end and leads His

[1] Church Missionary Society.

Southern Asia

world on into light, than that which His Son's disciples are supplying. He makes history none the less. Only toward that "far-off divine event, to which the whole creation moves," how much more speedily He could lead these people and lands if we would but turn in among them the mighty forces of His Gospel! "In Jerusalem the gate on Mount Moriah toward the Mount of Olives, is walled up to this hour," says Arnold, "because of the tradition that whenever a Christian shall pass through that gate, the Moslem religion and the Turkish Empire will come to an end." In this curious Moslem fancy there is this much truth, that it is in Christian hands to hasten or to retard that end,—for which

> "Christ also waits,
> But men are slow and late."

Arabia

Arabia is of little moment in present history. Its great deeds are done, and the noble chapters of its story were written centuries ago. A belt of unprogressive peoples on a narrow coast around hot, sandy plains—there is little more save here and there a fertile valley. All that has been said of the unprogressiveness of Islam, its sterility, its coldness, its corrupting influence taken in long history, holds with reference to Arabia. On the

Missions and Politics

east coast the slave trade still flourishes under the patronizing hypocrisy of the Sultan of Muscat, who is under the tutelage of France and Great Britain alike, and who, stripped of Zanzibar and nicely subsidized, appears outwardly respectable, and is usually peaceably quiet under the shadow of his old Portuguese forts. Twenty miles inland, however, the Sultan's writs run not. Outside of Muscat, quaint, romantic, mediæval, reminiscent of the old days when its wealth and the wealth of Ormuzd flowed to Ind, only two forces are disturbing Arabia. Along the East coast the Arabian Mission is working quietly, scattering the Scriptures and talking to men. And in the South, the Scotch Mission founded by Keith Falconer, is still carrying on the work which he laid down ten years ago, when like Valiant for Truth, his sword he gave to him that was to succeed him in his pilgrimage, and his courage and skill to him that could get it, while his marks and scars he carried with him, to be a witness for him that he had fought His battles who was then to be his Rewarder. "So he passed over and all the trumpets sounded for him on the other side."

The other force working in Arabia is the influence of Aden. From all around Somali-land,

Southern Asia

from Hadramant, from Yemen, from the countries all along the Red Sea, hundreds come to visit, and may be often heard, says General Haig,[1] "contrasting the two conditions—the peace, the order, the liberty, the just administration of the law, the religious toleration to be found in Aden, with the very reverse of all these things everywhere else. . . . Aden is known to the remotest corners (of Yemen) and the people are quietly drawing their own inferences and sometimes manifesting preferences which are evidently not a little irritating to the Turkish authorities."

That "neither Christianity nor Judaism ever struck deep root in the Arabian soil" as the great apologist for Islam says, "is true," but he adds, "the people were not suited to them, or they were not suited to the people. They lived on, on sufferance only, till a faith, which to the Arabs should be the more living one, should sweep them away." How long shall we let this challenge and condemnation stand? Whoever takes it up needs God with him; for man will be against him utterly.

India

From Mohammedanism under its own rulers,

[1] Sinker's *Memorial of Ion Keith Falconer*, pp. 142, 143, 229.

Missions and Politics

retrograding into the past beyond mediævalism, and crushing its few Christian subjects, to Mohammedanism under a Christian Empress, moving forward, educated, liberated and with no power to crush save by insurrection, is in time a long transition. In space, a few miles over the Arabian Sea opens the door of the new order. The waters were as light as a moonlit sky as we crossed one night last Spring, from Muscat to Kurrachee. The phosphorescence gleamed over the sea as a mystic fire. It rolled from the bows of the ship in great billows of emerald. Schools of fish broke it into constellations and Milky Ways. Flying things skimmed over it like rockets of ships in distress. The revolutions of the screw stood distinct in the sea like the coils of a great serpent, and the log line left a long luminous cut in the water astern. As we leaned on the rail and watched the play of light over the quiet sea, we looked back through the night to the dark lands we were leaving behind, and turned forward to those days of which Islam has never even prophesied, when

"All men's good
Is each man's rule, and universal love
Lies like a shaft of light across the land,
And like a lane of beams athwart the sea,
Through all the circle of the golden year."

Southern Asia

Is India indeed showing men the dawning of a new day for Asia, or the futility of all our hopes of it? Which? What it is teaching men, the lessons of God's shaping of its history and of the present unfolding of its mighty forces, is a study unsurpassed, surely, in human interest.

As an introduction to it and to a great deal else that is helpful to a man's understanding of this world and this day, I should like to suggest to you Professor Seeley's *Expansion of England*, a book that has done for England's political thinking, perhaps, what the author's other book, *Ecce Homo* did for England's theological thinking. Each book ran a plowshare through British conceptions, and made ready the beaten field for a fresh sowing and a larger reaping. Professor Seeley suggests much of what is said about India in this lecture. Many of the deeper meanings of the Queen's Anniversary were the fruits of Seeley's planting, nay rather of that divine planting that, mock as men often may, and despite its selfishness and disobedience, has been using the British race in a way unique and supreme.

Nowhere is this better illustrated than in India, where the presence of Great Britain in India, the way she came there, what she has been doing, and the fascinating issues of the future, constitute

Missions and Politics

as curious a problem as is to be found in history. The Holy Roman Empire was not more wonderful or significant. Indeed, if to the countries of the Roman Empire were added the whole of Germany, the Slavonic countries not included in Russia and Scandinavia, the resulting empire in population and extent would be but roughly equal to India. And Great Britain rules this. The most democratic and Christian of European powers has usurped the succession of the Great Mogul. "How can the same Nation," asks Seeley, "pursue two lines of policy so radically different without bewilderment, be despotic in Asia and democratic in Australia, be in the East at once the greatest Mussulman power in the world—ruling in Bengal over more Moslems than the Sultan has in his whole empire, the guardian of the property of thousands of idol temples, and at the same time, in the West be the foremost champion of free thought and spiritual religion; stand out as a great military imperialism to resist the march of Russia in Central Asia, at the same time that it fills Queensland and Manitoba with free settlers? Never certainly did any nation, since the world began, assume anything like so much responsibility." By assuming this responsibility Great Britain has become involved in all sorts of questions from

Southern Asia

which she would otherwise have been free. India and India almost alone has involved her in differences with Russia. No India, no Eastern Question. No Eastern Question—the whole history of the last two generations would have to be rewritten; who can speculate as to what their history would have been, with Egypt, Constantinople, Afghanistan, Burmah out of British politics?

And on the side of India this relationship is most interesting. It is scarcely accurate to say that it has been a conquest of India. There has been no spoliation nor any enslavement. India has not been tributary. Her taxes have been spent on herself. "The money drawn from India has been used in the government of India, and only that has been levied which was supposed to be needed for this purpose." Yet she has been subject to rulers who did not colonize her, but who made her freer than she had ever been before; who never maintained an army greater than 80,000 in number while they trained armies of her own people twice as great as their own; and whose whole number never sustained a greater proportion to the natives than one to one thousand; who tried to persuade her that they were leaving her old life unmolested, and only offering

Missions and Politics

her optional advantages, while they were in reality and in best of conscience hewing the very foundations away from all the old life and ways, and in matter of fact, from under their own position as rulers.

How did all this come about, and what is to be the end of it? It is a situation that will well repay analysis.

1. First, then, there never has been such a unity as India. The name has seemed to imply that there was an Indian nation and an Indian people, but in this it has been misleading. There is no common Indian *people*. There is, as the India Census Report says, a "heterogeneous mass that is known as the people of India"; but it is less one than the peoples of Europe. Formerly European writers divided the population into two races;—Hindu and Mohammedan; but as Sir Wm. Hunter points out, four well-marked elements are now recognized; first, "the non-Aryan tribes, called the Aborigines, and their half Hinduized descendants numbering about one-tenth of the population; second, the comparatively pure offspring of the Aryan or Sanscrit speaking race (the Brahmans or Rajputs) about the same in number; third, the great mixed population, known as the Hindus, which has grown out of

Southern Asia

the Aryan and non-Aryan elements (chiefly the latter), contributing two-thirds of the population; and fourth, the Mohammedans, numbering according to the census of 1890, 57,321,164. The ethnological history of India begins. where our vision ends, with a struggle between two races for the soil. One race had come in from West Central Asia and was of fair skin. The other race was dark and of lower type. The pure descendants of either race now nearly equal those of the other. Their mixed descendants constitute the great mass of the people, and a Moslem race from the Northwest supplied the other element."[1]

As there has not been since the dawn of this struggle in the dim past one Indian race, neither has there been one Indian *language*. The last Census returns not less than one hundred languages, two-thirds of the people speaking Aryo-Indic tongues, and one-fifth Dravidian, the rest being scattered among Kolarian, Aryo-Eranic, Tibeto-Burmah, Sinitic, etc. The Aryo-Indic tongues, Bengali, Marathi, Gujerathi, etc., though descendants of the ancient language, did not and do not constitute those who use them one people.

Nor had the people of India ever had, prior to British sovereignty, any common *national inter-*

---

[1] Hunter's *Indian Empire*, p. 68.

Missions and Politics

est. They had never been in the habit of forming a single whole in politics. There are dim traditions of this or that early king as having been lord of all India, but nothing ever as nearly approximated a common kingdom over all of India as the Mogul Emperors set up, and yet no one of them ever ruled over the whole of India. If we date the beginning of their empire from the capture of Lahore by Beber in 1524, it was not until 1594 that Akber had conquered Bengal and Sind and Gujerat, and so was king of Hindustan; and then none of the country to the South was his. The Nerbudda was his boundary. And only in 1683 was a great invasion of the Deccan made by Aurungzebe, while by that time the Mahratha power was already rising in the South, and in a generation the Mogul power began to decline. India was never a political unit.

Nor was India consolidated by a *common religion*. At first glance it would appear to be otherwise. Seventy-two per cent. of the population are returned by the Census as attached to the Brahmanic system, and looking back upon the assaults made on Brahmanism and the way they have been repulsed, it might be felt that in the matter of religion India is substantially one. But it must be noted on the other hand, that though

Southern Asia

the Buddhist revolt in the sixth century B. C., and the Greek invasions in the fourth century A. D. were both in the end overcome, they left their influence, as have the non-Aryan tribes and the non-Aryan low castes incorporated from them. All of these influences and "the reaction against the low beliefs, priestly oppressions and bloody rites which resulted from the compromise between Brahmanism and aboriginal worship," which received special impetus from Sankar Acharja who founded the great Sivaite sect about 700 A. D., had rent Hinduism into sections before the influence of Western education and religion crashed against its foundations with the impetus of God. While Brahmanism contained the germ perhaps of a common nationality, its weakness was shown in its practically making room for Mohammedanism, which refused to be assimilated in easy compliance with the loose compromising ways of Hinduism. Islam came challenging racial, political, religious, linguistic antipathy. Brahmanism did not have spirit to express itself in patriotism. Nor did it even when the Mahratha power under the control of the Brahman caste arose in Central India. In Brahmanism itself there has been neither the power nor the reality of unity. Moreover, out-

Missions and Politics

side of strict Brahmanism, Buddhism has left the Jain sect, numbering 1,416,638 now, who "deny the authority of the Veda, . . . disregard sacrifice, practise a strict morality, believe that their past and their future states depend upon their own actions rather than on any external deity, and scrupulously reverence the vital principle in man and beast."[1] Besides the Jains, the Sikhs have arisen to augment the want of external unity, but warring not against Hindus so much as against Islam; while to all of this confusion, the Mussulmans are added. In 712 the young Kasim secured foothold in Sind which the Hindus did not regain until 828. Mahmoud of Ghazni, however, fixed the yoke securely in 1001, and the house of Ghor, the Slave Kings, the Sayids and the Moguls, with lesser men, brought the Moslem dynasties down to the beginning of this century. In no regard, therefore,—race, language, government or religion, was India a common nation.[2] It had no sense of unity or consciousness of nationality.

2. Secondly, it was because India had no sense of unity or consciousness of nationality that the Indian peoples passed so easily under

---
[1] Hunter's *Indian Empire*, p. 155.
[2] *India Census, 1891, General Report*, chap. v., pp. 121-208.

the government of the British Empire. The land was a jarring, warring tangle of native states and seditions and corruptions, lush as a great jungle, when the French and the English began the rivalry of trade. The East India Company came into existence in 1600, and it was created solely for the purpose of trade. War with the native states was not thought of at all; and when more than a century later it was thought of, it was not for territorial aggrandizement, but in support of trade. In 1748 the Company undertook, owing to disturbances in the Deccan, the functions of war and government. It was not the will of the directors of the Company to create an Empire. The Empire came into existence through forces overruling their will, against which they struggled in vain. Even the idea of armed interference was not original with them. Dupleix, the Frenchman, made the two discoveries that led to the conquest, if it may be so called, of India, "1. The weakness of the native armies against European discipline. 2. The facility of imparting that discipline to natives in the European service," and Dupleix began European Empire in India when acting on these principles he interfered in the war of succession in Hyderabad that broke out on the death of the great Nizam ul Mulk in 1748, and so hoped to gain the balance of power. The Company took up arms first to defend its fortunes and then to spread its trade, by widening its influence and pacifying society. It was not a war to conquer or subdue a nation. The idea of a British army of a few hundred men conquering India, or of 80,000 men holding now 296,000,000 in subjection is absurd. The conquest was an internal revolution in Indian society, rather than an external invasion of one State upon another. India presented no united character. It had been ruled in sections by foreigners. Many of its people were foreigners. The British conquered by means of native armies. Absolute political deadness ruled in the whole country. For centuries before the British came, the great governments were alien,—Moslem. The State rested on power or skill; not on right or sense of nationality. There was no patriotism. It was by taking advantage of this absence of national unity and by playing section against section that a little handful of Englishmen became masters of the whole country.

It soon passed out of the hands of private individuals organized as a trading company into the hands of the British Empire. For though the East India Company was a private concern, and

Southern Asia

in 1765 nominally held office under the Empire of the Great Mogul, it had been recognized in the British Parliament, yes at once asserted, that whatever territorial acquisitions the Company made were under the control of Parliament, though Parliament never asked consent of the Great Mogul. The Company in his service took provinces, submitted them to the control of Great Britain, and when in 1858 the Company was abolished its vast possessions passed under the British Crown.

The Company was a trading company. It engaged in war and took lands and kingdoms for the advantage of its trade. Under Hastings a mere spirit of rapacity hurried on the conquest. Later, under Lord Wellesley, Great Britain began to see what a vast trust was given to her, and the theory of intervention and annexation was deliberately laid down. Lord Dalhousie carried it forward with a high and violent hand. Small men played their part. Save for the trade, Great Britain would over and over again have lamented her responsibility, and doubtless would have dropped it. When India cannot pay all her own expenses, and ceases to be profitable as a field for trade, England will withdraw as soon as possible. Let those who think her too high-minded and unselfish for this, remember Khartoum and the fall of Chinese Gordon.[1] But none the less, above all elements of national glory and purely selfish trade, a high-minded recognition of a great purpose in being thus charged with the education of a nation embracing one-fifth of the human race, has had its place in the sober thinking of the British Empire.

In nothing has this spirit been better shown than in the tremendous work Great Britain has done toward creating that very sense of national unity and power which would have rendered absolutely impossible the establishment of British dominion if it had been in existence when that dominion was imposed. The old India was rent into little kingdoms and tribes. The new is one of the most highly centralized governments on earth. While fine roads and railroads are binding the country ever closer together. The opening of the civil service to natives schools them deeply in the idea of national unity. The great educational system of the Empire trains thousands of the young men of India, giving them all that Europe has. They know the history of India, the principles of political science, the rela-

---

[1] "Foreigners do not appear to realize the business view we take of war as of other matters where our business interests are concerned. Our conduct is regulated mainly by business considerations."—London *Times*, quoted in London despatch to New York *Sun*, March 10, 1898.

Southern Asia

tive dimensions of nations, their populations and resources and relations. The relations of India to England they well understand, on what the British possession rested, and on what it rests. They know the movements of Russia and their relation to the future of Asia. They have their English and vernacular press. A great body of public opinion is growing up. They know that the world speaks of India as a unity. They know that Great Britain deals with India as a unity. The sense of unity, of nationality is developing. From the day British power began to establish everywhere order, law, trade, education, it was inevitable that this should be the result.

3. India was not a nation. Therefore Great Britain conquered it and has held it. Great Britain is making it a nation. What will be the result? Twenty years ago the shrewdest students of history were saying this: "If there could arise in India a nationality movement similar to that . . . in Italy, the English Power would not even make the resistance that was made in Italy by Austria, but must succumb at once. . . . If the feeling of a common nationality began to exist there only feebly—if without inspiring any active desire to drive out the foreigner, it only created a notion that it was shameful to assist

Missions and Politics

him in maintaining his dominion—from that day almost our Empire would cease to exist; for of the army by which it is garrisoned, two-thirds consist of native soldiers." This feeling is absent; there is no love of independence because it presupposes a political consciousness that is lacking. "Long submission makes the people passively tolerant of any Government. The people of India are satisfied with ours." The Mutiny was wholly an army movement and was subdued by using the people of India themselves against it. "So long as that can be done," went on the students of twenty years ago, "and so long as the population has not formed the habit of criticising their Government, whatever it may be, and of rebelling against it, the government of India from England is possible. . . . On the other hand, if this feeling ever does spring up, if India does begin to breathe as a single national whole—and our own rule is perhaps doing more than ever was done by former governments to make this possible,—then . . . the feeling would soon gain the native army, and on the native army we ultimately depend . . . and the moment a mutiny is but threatened which shall be no mere mutiny but the expression of a universal feeling of nationality, at that moment all hope is at

Southern Asia

an end, as all desire ought to be at an end, of preserving our Empire. For we are not really conquerors of India, and we cannot rule her as conquerors; if we undertook to do so, it is not necessary to inquire whether we could succeed, for we should assuredly be ruined financially by the mere attempt."[1]

No shrewder forecast could have been made. But it reaches far on into the future. There is as yet no universal feeling of nationality. Religious feud between Moslem and Hindu is still a bar to unity. Large classes are interested in the maintenance of the present order. And national pride, trade interests, and the momentum of tradition would lead Great Britain to crush any present mutiny as effectually as the Sepoy Rebellion.

Nevertheless, the murmurs of discontent were never louder than at the present time, and they are, in the main, expressions of the growing national sentiment of the people, though each complaint or stir of excitement springs out of its own conditions. As Sir Richard Temple has pointed out, "The peace and security (and justice,) introduced and maintained (by the British Government) closes many avenues against restless ambi-

[1] Seeley's *Expansion of England*, pp. 262, 263.

Missions and Politics

tion, shuts off many careers of enterprise and adventure, wrecks the self-reliance, stifles the aspirations and deadens the energies of many"[1] used to the lax rules of politics and gain which are allowed elsewhere to control in Asiatic life. The village peasantry have gained greatly in the establishment of order and quiet, and to some extent of honesty; but below the superficial crust of British influence, the old tides run dark and strong still, and these village people most benefited are the fanatics in religion, while of short memory, slight gratitude and great ignorance of history and the world. The educated natives are the men who voice the complaints in congresses, on the platform, and in the press. Hungry for office they grudge the British civilian his position and authority, and overcrowd the professions. The true Hindus despise sincerely their British rulers, look contemptuously upon their cut and dried scientific knowledge, arid and uninteresting beside their own rich reverie and the luxury of their unbounded speculation, and long for their old Oriental ways. The dominant attitude of the British nettles the Hindu into hatred. Moreover, all the efforts of the Government to elevate the lower classes, who do not appreciate

[1] Temple's *India in 1880*, p. 107.

Southern Asia

being elevated, tend to depress in comparison those higher classes who once ruled the land, monopolizing the posts of office and growing rich out of rule. The agitating class denounces British rule as impoverishing, sapping the life from the land. They declare that pensions to retired British officers amount to more than all the salaries paid to active native office-holders. "India for Indians," they cry—a shout of nationalism arising at last. It does not avail to point out that under the Mogul Empire, 1593-1761, the tax returns were sixty millions sterling a year, while for the ten years ending 1879, under the British Empire in India, with a far larger population and territory, the returns were only on the average thirty-five millions, nor to say that under the former the land tax was nearly twice what it was under the latter, and that the rates are far less than in Japan. Why will these answers not suffice? Because the sense of nationality is developing. Good government, famine relief, the most heroic and self-sacrificing efforts to delay and to slay the bubonic plague— these instead of calling forth complete loyalty, are now made the grounds of fresh agitation and the pretext even of riot and assassination.[1]

[1] Monier Williams' *Modern India*, pp. 176-179, 343-365.

Missions and Politics

Among the Moslems of late things have been even worse. The victories of Turkey in Greece have stirred the Moslem world not with devotion to the Sultan as caliph, though that might come if it were safe and could be shown to be to the interest of all, but to the military mission of Islam. Sir William Hunter names one of the chapters of his book on *Our Indian Mussulmans*, "The Chronic Conspiracy within our Territory," referring to the incessant agitation kept up by the Wahabi preachers calling the faithful to a holy war, and so constantly rousing the class which lost most by the British Power, the class of proudest memories, and of most virile religious life. The leader of the Wahabi movement in India was Sayid Ahmad, who in 1826, preached a Jehad against the Sikhs. Ever since, the Wahabis have been preaching not treason, but doctrines which lead to it, and with what political instigation it is impossible to say. And last year some mollah, called mad, contributed largely to the troubles on the Northwest frontier, by his wild exhortations ; the chronic panic fear of the British Nation lest the route of the Khyber Pass, which since Mahmud of Ghazni, has been the beaten road of invasion, and the only point where India is vulnerable by land, should be in some way betrayed into hostile control, furnishing the best of fuel for a conflagration, and fuel always available for Moslem agitators.

Thus all that Great Britain has done to unify India, to supply education and political vitality, even the purely beneficent blessings of charity, and especially the attempt to keep India inviolate by shady diplomatic deals with the Amir of Afghanistan and war beyond Peshawur have served merely to develop and strengthen a national consciousness and a sense of revolt against Western rule among the increasing disaffected classes.

4. Fourthly: The one element which in the education of India would have averted the perils now to be faced, the British Government did not supply. For a long while indeed, the East India Company studiously set itself to prevent the entrance into India of this element. The Company desired "to keep India wholly as a kind of inviolate paradise," and strove to shut out all that was European save trade. Even if the Company had succeeded in this, and had been followed in the same policy by Great Britain, trade and unity of government would have produced the sense of unity, of nationality, though far more slowly, which has now been produced, and would have done so without the element of Christianity, of

Missions and Politics

Christian understanding, and of confidence, to rob it of its great dangers.

About 1813, the change came by which the old idea that only trade was legitimate was abandoned. It had been deemed lawful to murder, bribe, steal, corrupt and wage war for the sake of trade, but to use the advantages so gained for the sake of teaching the people, giving them the ideas and life of the West, was supposed to involve a breach of some sort of tacit contract with the natives, by which, if they would be good, and be ruled and buy British articles, the British would let them worship idols and kill their children and burn their widows, and otherwise be as heathen as they might wish. When, however, the Company's charter was renewed in 1813, it was directed to appropriate a sum for education and the introduction of useful sciences.

The question at once arose, however, as to whether such education and sciences were to be given according to Oriental ideas by the rulers as in sort the trustees of the heathenism of the land, or according to Western ideas and the spirit of civilization. Macaulay was in India when this question was decided, and he wrote the minute that was adopted. The decision was in favor of an education toward civilization. That was right.

Southern Asia

Under the powerful support of Duff, it was also in favor of the making of English the base of the education. Which was wrong and absurd, as the British Government saw when Sir Charles Wood sent his dispatch of 1854 which gave the vernacular some just recognition. Since then, the British Government has discharged with tremendous energy the work of introducing Western notions of the universe, Western science and learning. But all this work has been directed rather at instruction, improvement, than at moulding of character; and it has led hundreds away from humble trades to seek government appointment or the status of petty gentlemen. As Sir Monier Williams said, "We teach a native to believe in himself. We deprecate his not desiring to be better than his fathers. . . . We puff him up with an overweening opinion of his own sufficiency. We inflate him with a sublime sense of his own importance as a distinct unit in the body politic. We reveal to him the meaning of 'I am,' 'I can,' 'I will,' 'I shall,' 'I know,' without inculcating any lesson of 'I ought' and 'I ought not,' without implanting any sense of responsibility to and dependence on an Eternal, Almighty and All-wise Being for life, for strength, for knowledge—without in short, imparting real

Missions and Politics

self-knowledge, or teaching true self-mastery, or instilling high principles and high motives. Such a system carries with it its own nemesis."[1]

On the fundamental weakness here, Sir Herbert Edwardes, one of the finest administrators ever in India, laid his hand thirty years ago, "That secular education and civilization will ever regenerate a nation I do not believe. It does not go to the root of the matter. It is a police force at best. It does much to suppress crime between man and man, but it does nothing for sin between man and his Maker. Undoubtedly it softens what is brutal in human nature, but it leaves untouched what is Satanic. It was well said by one of the ablest missionaries in India, that 'He alone can make a new nation who can form a new man.'"[2]

That is what England has been doing in India —forming a new nation on the structure and with the power of national unity, but without real life or the sense of Divine duty. It has been a perilous procedure. "I believe," said Lord Lawrence, "that what more tended to stir up the Indian Mutiny than any one thing was, the habitual cowardice of Great Britain as to her

---

[1] Monier Williams' *Modern India*, p. 304.
[2] Young's *Success of Christian Missions*, pp. 73, 74.

own religion. It led many to think her atheistical and so not to be trusted; and others to believe that under a veil of indifference she hid some deep scheme to make India Christian."

Of course the position taken has been that England could not teach Christianity; she had no right, and to do it would have confounded spiritual with secular and worldly motives. But she has never scrupled to teach against Christianity in her schools, and atheism and agnosticism have been openly taught. Lord Lawrence held other views. "In doing the best we can for the people," he said, in 1858, in his dispatches as Chief Commissioner of the Punjab, "we are bound by *our* conscience and not by theirs. . . . To say that we have no right to offer Christian teaching to government schools because we do not allow the native religions to be taught there, is to misapprehend the fundamental relation that in this country subsists between the Government and the people. We are to do the best we can for them, according to our lights and they are to obey us."[1] Lawrence's views did not prevail because there were few Lawrences. And Great Britain has gone on unifying India and making it dangerous, filling it with trained and inflammable

[1] Young's *Success of Christian Missions*, pp. 80-82.

Missions and Politics

men devoid of moral foundations, but not supplying the one force that would make these things blessings and not a curse.

Not to press this further, I may only quote the corroborating judgment of one of the latest travellers, Mr. Julian Hawthorne. "The only salvation of India even from an economic point of view, in the opinion of those who have longest and most deeply studied it is its Christianization. . . . Let England inspire India with a veritable Christian faith, and nine-tenths of the present difficulties would spontaneously cease. But in order to inspire such faith, we must first possess it; and England, conscientious, energetic, just and proud of her religious history, is not a Christian nation, and therefore forfeits the measureless power for good which might otherwise be hers."

5. And now, fifthly, that which the British Government in India has not done, which indeed it at the first malignantly opposed, has always professedly treated with neutrality, and in its educational system has antagonized and counteracted, and which yet was the only hope and salvation of the British Power itself in India, the missionary work has been doing. It has been supplying the force that would rob national

Southern Asia

unity of its peril, and make of India not the irritable, mutinous foe but the hearty, sound-souled ally of the British Empire. There have been English statesmen who saw this. Viscount Halifax, Secretary of State for India, declared forty-three years ago, "No person can be more anxious to promote the spread of Christianity in India than we are. Independently of Christian considerations, I believe that every additional Christian in India is an additional bond of union with this country, and an additional source of strength to the Empire." "It is our interest," said Palmerston, then Prime Minister, "to promote the diffusion of Christianity as far as possible throughout the length and breadth of India."[1] These were politicians' views. The matter was more broadly treated nearly a generation ago by one of the keenest students of this great problem, who then said, "Is it conceivable that some day we may find our Christianity a reconciling element between ourselves and the contending religions, (and the nationality movement growing up in India)? . . . We are to remember that, as Islam is the crudest expression of Semitic religion, Brahmanism on the other hand is an expression of Aryan thought. Now among the religions of the

[1] Young's *Success of Christian Missions*, p. 88.

Missions and Politics

world Christianity stands out as a product of the fusion of Semitic with Aryan ideas. It may be said that India and Europe in respect of religion have both the same elements, but that in India the elements have not blended, while in England they have resulted in Christianity. Judaism and classical Paganism were in Europe at the beginning of our era what Mohammedanism and Brahmanism are now in India; but in India the elements have remained separate and have made only occasional efforts to unite, as in the Sikh religion and in the religion of Akber. In Europe a great fusion took place by means of the Christian Church, which fusion has throughout modern history been growing more and more complete."[1] Will Christianity once more work a great absorption and regeneration of this character for the redemption and cleansing of India, and so save it though unified and nationalized?

Great as these charges laid on Christianity are, the Mission work which has been its deposit and factor, has been magnificently bearing them. Even the report to Parliament of a Secretary of State for India, (1872–1873), has recognized this, and declared, Its institutions "augur well for the future moral progress of the native population of

[1] Seeley's *Expansion of England*, p. 323.

Southern Asia

India, from these signs of solid advance already exhibited on every hand, and gained within the brief period of two generations. This view of the general influence of their teaching, and of the greatness of the revolution which it is silently producing, is not taken by missionaries only. It has been accepted by many distinguished officers of the Government, and has been emphatically endorsed by the high authority of Sir Bartle Frere. Without pronouncing an opinion on the matter, the Government of India cannot but acknowledge the great obligations under which it is laid by the benevolent exertions made by the (600) missionaries, whose blameless examples and self-denying exertions, are infusing new vigor into the stereotyped life of the great populations placed under English rule, and are preparing them to be in every way better men and better citizens of the great Empire in which they dwell."

Those who have been responsible for the Government of India have not been deluded by any idea that Missions have failed. They know full well that they are constructing the firmest foundations on which British influence in India can rest, and are reaching down to those classes for whose mental and moral improvement the Government has been able to do the least. They

Missions and Politics

know that they are giving character to such of the higher educated classes as possess it, and are teaching temperateness, sound judgment, and that just sense of responsibility which should accompany the spirit of independence, to more thousands than are awed by the army or subsidized by the gift of government appointment. If out of all the perils of its great experiment in India the British Government should emerge peacefully, it will be because Christian Missions have laid in India the foundations of that kingdom of righteousness that cannot be moved; while, as for India herself, where formerly

> " Midnight hushed the world
> Save where the beasts of darkness in the brake
> Crept and cried out, as fear and hatred cry,
> As vice and avarice and anger creep
> In the black jungle of man's ignorance,"

the same Missions are bringing the hour when

> "High as the herald star which fades in floods
> Of silver, warming into pale gold, caught
> By topmost clouds, and flowing on their rims
> To fervent glow, flushed from the brink
> With saffron, scarlet, crimson, amethyst;
> Whereat the sky burns splendid to the blue,
> And, robed in raiment of glad light, the King
> Of light and glory cometh." [1]

Indo-China

I have left myself scant space in which to speak of Indo-China, the third of the protruding

[1] Arnold's *Light of Asia*.

Southern Asia

peninsulas of South Asia, but Indo-China has no separate destiny. Slowly from Sir Stamford Raffles' settlement at Singapore and from Assam, the British influence stole Eastward; while from Tonquin and Cambodia the French have crept Westward. The old fiction of the necessity of a buffer state, indeed of all buffer states, has been gradually disappearing, as no states but the buffer states have been left to be seized; and Siam crushed between England and France is being slowly absorbed. It is only a question of time now until the boundary lines of French and British territory shall meet, and the mountain range which runs as a spine through the centre of Siam, constitute their line of division. All West of the line will share the destiny of the India Empire, and all East will pass under the curious colonial system of France;—curious because it is so difficult to understand why God allows such a poor travesty upon His earth.

In the matter of virility and fanatical conviction Siam is at the opposite pole from Arabia. It has an enlightened king, most kindly disposed to missionary influence, and wholly favorable to civilization; but the people are without power, aspiration or vital force. Centuries of Buddhism

Missions and Politics

have emasculated them. When all that is claimed for primitive Buddhism is granted, its proclamation of peace and good-will and brotherhood, its avowed sympathy with social liberty and freedom, its teaching of self-denial without torture, its inculcation of charity, generosity, broadness, tolerance and love, its advocacy of respect for life and compassion toward all creatures, it yet remains true that it has left the nations it touched as weak as it found them, if it has not weakened them yet more, has held no stimulating tonic of purity and progress for its followers, has never produced any great literature or art, has been associated with no great historic movements, has developed the most ignorant priesthood, the most mechanical worship, and the most prolific and absurd idolatry, has shown itself in reality atheistic and barren of all authority and dominion. "I have neither the time nor the inclination to describe to you the hideousness that came in its wake," said Swami Vivakananda recently in Madras, "the most hideous ceremonies, the most horrible, the most obscene books that human hand ever wrote or the human brain ever conceived, the most bestial forms that ever passed under the name of religion have all been the creation of degraded Buddhism." I am not sure

Southern Asia

that Buddhism deserves this palm over Hinduism, but it may be.

In the midst of this enervating jungle, the clean, vitalizing work of the Gospel stands out wholesomely. It has but begun, but its power for the final good is as a flood compared with all other. As a Bengal Civil Service official wrote of the Karens, "Nothing that the Government has yet done has succeeded in rousing the people to a sense of their dignity as men or as a nation. The Government has given them nothing around which their national aspirations could rally. Christianity at the hands of the American missionaries has done this. Once a village has embraced Christianity, it feels itself head and shoulders above its neighbors, and all the energies of the people are employed in making this village worthy of the name. No labor, no expense are spared. The Christian village must be clean, healthy, neat; it must have the best school and the best church they can afford. They will not have anything but the best."[1]

And this is the drift everywhere. God has caught these Nations in the sweep of a mighty history. He is making it fast under our eyes and the great force which He is using, greater I be-

Young's *Success of Christian Missions*, p. 127

lieve, than those political forces which He is as surely also guiding, is the Christian Church, with its power of transformation, of life, as fresh and vigorous as when it poured new from the bleeding Lamb on Calvary. Even now,

> "The hands upon that cruel tree
> Extended wide as mercy's span
> Are gathering to the Son of Man,
> The ages past and yet to be."

All the other forces at work are puny compared with His. Can Buddhism compare? Who holds it only or consistently? Not one. "Not one," says Rhys Davids, "of the 500,000,000 who offer flowers now and then on Buddhist shrines, who are more or less molded by Buddhist teaching, is only or altogether a Buddhist."[1] Can Hinduism compare? "I must tell you in plain words," declared one of its smoothest prophets recently to his people, "we are weak, very weak. . . . We have lost faith. Would you believe me, we have less faith than the English men and women, thousand times less faith! These are plain words, but I must say them. . . . Your blood, . . . your brain, . . . your body is weak. You talk of reform, of ideals, and all these for the last one hundred years; and when it comes to practice, you are

[1] Rhys Davids' *Buddhism*, p. 7.

not to be found anywhere; so that you have disgusted the whole world, and the very name of reform is a thing of ridicule to the whole world. The only cause is that you are weak, weak, weak; your body is weak, your mind is weak! You have no faith in yourselves. . . . Our capitals are filled with the most rotten superstitions in the world." Can government compare? "The white invasion," wrote Julian Hawthorne, "has done India good just in measure as it has been accompanied by genuine religious influence. So far as it has been commercial and indifferent merely, it has done harm. England has unselfishly done for India more, I think, than any other nation would do, but she had failed to give her an upward impulse."

"The Lord of all creatures, . . . the King of the day of judgment . . . the most high, who hath created and completely formed His creatures and who determineth them to various ends and directeth them to attain the same," is using all of these forces, but His force is mightier than these. Beside it, they

> "Stand on as feeble feet
> As frailty doth and only great do seem
> To little minds that do them so esteem."

Beside them, it stands calm, unobtrusive, but doing its work with a solidity, a penetration, an energy which prove it to be to-day, as of old, the power of God unto the redemption of a world. And over the strife and storm and clangor of the fearful struggle that is shaking these lands, whoso has ears to hear can catch its voice, clear and commanding as the voice of its Master amid the waves on Gennesaret.

LECTURE III

China

"*States!*" *I said;* "*why, what simplicity is this, that you should use the term 'State' of any but our own State! Other States may indeed be spoken of more grandiloquently in the plural number, for they are many in one—a game of cities at which men play.* . . . "

" . . . . *Beginning with the assumption that our State if rightly ordered is perfect.*"

"*That is most certain.*"

"*And being perfect, our State is wise and valiant and temperate and just.*"

"*That is also clear.*"

PLATO, *The Republic.*

LECTURE III

CHINA

"THERE are men of that tyrannical school who say that China is not fit to sit at the council board of the Nations, who call them barbarians, who attack them on all occasions with a bitter and unrelenting spirit," said Anson Burlingame in New York, on June 23, 1868, when he was representing the Chinese Government as head of the Embassy which introduced China to the Western world when at last the long closed doors were forced open. And "these things," continued Burlingame, "I utterly deny. I say on the contrary, that that is a great and noble people. It has all the elements of a splendid nationality. It has the most numerous people on the face of the globe; it is the most homogeneous people in the world; its language is spoken by more human beings than any other in the world, and it is written in the rock; it is a country where there is a greater unification of thought than in any other country in the world; it is a country where the maxims of the great sages, coming down memo-

Missions and Politics

rized, have permeated the whole people until their knowledge is rather an instinct than an acquirement. It is a people loyal while living, and whose last prayer when dying is to sleep in the sacred soil of their fathers. It is a land of scholars and of schools—a land of books, from the smallest pamphlet up to voluminous encyclopedias. It is a land, sir, as you have said, where the privileges are common; it is a land without caste for they destroyed their feudal system two thousand one hundred years ago, and they built up their great structure of civilization on the great idea that the people are the source of power. That idea was uttered by Mencius two thousand years ago, and it was old when he uttered it. The power flows forth from that people into practical government through the coöperative system, and they make scholarship a test of merit. I say it is a great, a polite, a patient, a sober and an industrious people; and it is such a people as this, that the bitter boor would exclude from the council hall of the Nations. It is such a Nation as this that the tyrannical element would put under the ban. They say that all these people (a third [!] of the human race) must become the weak wards of the West; wards of Nations not so populous as many of their provinces; wards

China

of people who are younger than their newest village in Manchuria. I do not mean to say that the Chinese are perfect; far from it. They have their faults, their pride and their prejudices like other people. These are profound and they must be overcome. They have their conceits like other people, and they must be done away; but they are not to be removed by talking to them with cannon, by telling them that they are feeble and weak, and that they are barbarians."[1]

With these fair words from our countryman of florid speech, the most impressive and curious nation on the earth was introduced to national intercourse with other peoples. She had been talked to with cannon. Otherwise she would have continued to refuse introduction. But the persuasive iron speech of the Opium and Arrow Wars was seductive and the mighty people came out of their seclusion.

I have called China impressive, curious and mighty. These three adjectives belong to China and they belong in the same degree to no other people.

The Chinese people are a mighty people. The idea that they were mighty in war was finally abandoned three years ago, but until the army

---

[1] Nevius's *China and the Chinese*, p. 453.

Missions and Politics

and navy of Japan showed how hollow and vain were all the Chinese military and naval pretensions, China was reckoned a sleeping giant who had been not inactively preparing even in sleep for future struggle. Had not Chinese armies conquered the whole heart of Asia? Had they not driven Russia out of the region South of the Amoor? Had they not held the dependencies against all foes? Had they not made the French war in Tonquin a scandal and almost a shame to France? No testing had ever come. What China was or could do was enfolded in mystery. It is not strange that Great Britain looked upon her as her best ally against Russian aggression, and that all the politics of the East turned upon the conviction of China's formidable character as a warlike nation. All this is past now, and the Western people smile at their folly in having been so deceived, and sneer at the pathetic weakness of the Celestial Giant. But this is after the narrow judgment of men whose gods are made of saber slashes and running blood. China's unfitness for the modern science of butchery which we call war, and her weakness in such work, while manifesting the radical defects of incapacity for organization and exact obedience, but bring into clearer relief her mighty adaptation to the

China

arts of peace, and her genuine power in those spheres which I confess seem to me better spheres for the exercise of power than the fields of organized murder or national land robbery or the lust of pride.

In the more worthy regards China is a mighty nation. No people are more frugal, more contented, more orderly, more patient, more industrious, more filial and respectful among themselves. "They have been for ages the great centre of light and civilization in Central and Eastern Asia. They have given literature and religion to the millions of Korea and Japan." Even a generation of Western civilization has not shaken Chinese influence off the thought and politics and ethics of Japan. Printing originated with the Chinese, and was used by them hundreds of years before it was known in the West. The magnetic needle, gunpowder, silk fabrics, chinaware and porcelain were old tales with the Chinese before our civilization began. Our latest ideas were wrought out by the Chinese ages ago,—Civil Service examinations and assignment of office for merit and tested capacity, trades unions and organizations, the sense of local responsibility in municipal administration. Already numbering one-fourth the population of the earth, China ought to be able,

Missions and Politics

Dr. Faber says,[1] "comfortably to support at least five times the number of its present inhabitants," taking Germany as a basis of judgment, for the average population of Germany is three times denser than the average population of China, and China's physical and climatic conditions are more favorable than those of Germany, while the Chinese are more frugal than the Germans. In business, manufactures or trade no other people can compete with the Chinese on equal terms. Wherever equal terms prevail, they are driving the foreign merchants out of their markets and ports, and make other labor impossible. And when, as is sure to happen, their own or foreign capitalists drawing raw materials from China, manufacture their cottons, iron, silk, woolens and merchandise in Chinese mills with Chinese labor, those who now regard these Chinese as weak because they cannot fight with guns and ships will recognize that there are other standards than these by which the power of a people is to be gauged.

Perhaps one reason why the Chinese have been so underjudged and certainly one reason for the attitude of contempt and ridicule civilized nations have ever taken toward them is found in their curious peculiarities; for they are, as has been said,

[1] Faber's *China in the Light of History*, p. 2.

the most curious of peoples. But another reason is found in our misunderstanding of them. As Dr. Martin once said, "They are denounced as stolid, because we are not in possession of a medium sufficiently transparent to convey our ideas to them or to transmit theirs to us; and stigmatized as barbarians, because we want the breadth to comprehend a civilization different from our own. They are represented as servile imitators, though they have borrowed less than any other people; as destitute of the inventive faculty, though the world is indebted to them for a long catalogue of the most useful discoveries; and as clinging with unquestioning tenacity to a heritage of traditions, though they have passed through many and profound changes in the course of their history."[1] And we have misunderstood the Chinese in this way not because of any want of will to understand them, but because from our point of view the Chinese character and mind are so perplexing, almost inexplicable. Some have even denied in their confusion that there is a common character or mind. Mr. Henry Norman in *Peoples and Politics of the Far East*, has done so, contending that there is no real unity in China; but those who know China better, hold a differ-

---

[1] Martin's *The Chinese*, p. 228.

ent view. "China is not," one of them declares, "an immense congeries of polyps each encased in his narrow cell, a workshop and a tomb, and all toiling on without the stimulus of common sympathy or mental reaction. China is not . . . like British India, an assemblage of tribes with little or no community of feeling. It is a unit, and through all its members there sweeps the mighty tide of a common life."[1]

And yet no one has ever described this life. Those who have come nearest to doing so have confessed their failure. They have hit off characteristics but not the character. Mr. Smith frankly calls his book which is the best account of Chinese character we have *Chinese Characteristics*, and one of the fairest as well as shrewdest writers on China, Mr. George Wingrove Cooke, the special correspondent of the London *Times*, with Lord Elgin's Mission, doubted whether the Chinese could be understood and described by the Western mind. "I have in these letters," he wrote, "introduced no elaborate essay upon Chinese character. It is a great omission. . . . The truth is that, I have written several very fine characters for the whole Chinese race, but having the misfortune to have

[1] Martin's *The Chinese*, p. 229.

the people under my eye at the same time with my essay, they were always saying something or doing something which rubbed so rudely against my hypothesis, that in the interest of truth I burned several successive letters. I may add that I have often talked over this matter with the most eminent and candid sinologues, and have always found them ready to agree with me as to the impossibility of a Western mind forming a conception of Chinese character as a whole. These difficulties, however, occur only to those who know the Chinese practically; a smart writer entirely ignorant of his subject might readily strike off a brilliant and antithetical analysis, which should leave nothing to be desired but truth."[1]

Who of us, for example, can honestly appreciate or understand the point of view of a people among whom human life is regarded as these illustrations show? A man throws himself into a canal and is dragged out. But not to be frustrated in this way, simply sits down on the bank and starves himself to death to be revenged against somebody who has cheated him and whose good name will be tarnished in this way. One day, as a Chinese paper relates, a sow be-

[1] Cooke's *China*, p. 7.

Missions and Politics

longing to a Mrs. Feng, happening to knock down and slightly injure the front door of a Mrs. Wang, the latter at once proceeded to claim damages, which were refused. Whereupon a fierce altercation ensued, which terminated in Mrs. Wang's threatening to take her own life. Mrs. Feng, upon hearing of this direful threat, resolved at once to steal a march upon her enemy by taking her own life, and so bringing trouble and discredit upon Mrs. Wang. She accordingly threw herself into the canal. And these are not uncommon or forced illustrations. They are part of the common routine of life.[1]

And the occasional cruelty of the Chinese is beyond belief. "I know of a case in a wealthy Mandarin's family," writes one old missionary, "where the only grown daughter showing signs of leprosy, a slave girl was bought and butchered, and the patient fed with the flesh of the poor victim."[2] How is this to be understood among a people of high moral standards, and ancient and boasted civilization?

And their government contains equally curious features; men appointed to expensive office without salary and then punished for squeezing; lofty

---

[1] Norman's *Peoples and Politics of the Far East*, p. 278.
[2] Faber's *Famous Women of China*, p. 4.

China

political ethics combined with the most corrupt official class in the world; vast numbers of eunuchs, 3,000 in the palace of the Emperor alone, under a system which proclaims the sonless man to be an outcast soul, doomed eternally; a professed atheism, or at best agnosticism combined with the most silly superstitions. This, for example, is one of the decrees for the year 1896, taken from the *Imperial Gazette*, "A shroud inscribed with the T'olo prayers, the work of the Tibetan Buddhist Pontiff, is granted to the deceased noble Tsai Tsin." This is another of less recent date: "Tso Tsung t'ang refers for favorable consideration an application made to him that a certain girl who died in 1469 may be canonized. Wherever rain has failed, prayers offered up at the shrine of the girl angel at Pa-mi-shan have usually been successful. An inquiry into the earthly history of the girl angel shows that she was born in the capital of Kansuh, and during her childhood lived an exemplary life. She was guiltless of a smile or any sort of levity; but, on the contrary, spent the livelong day in doing her duty. Arrived at maidenhood, her mother wished to betroth her, but the girl refused to marry, and betook herself to the Pa-mi hills, where she gave herself up to religious exercise and nourished herself on spiritual food, until she was transformed into an angel. After she had left this world, the people of the locality found that an appeal to her was invariably answered, and a temple was built in her honor. During the recent dry season, prayers for rain were always granted, thus showing that though hundreds of years have gone by, the maiden still watches over the locality. The memorialist is of opinion that she may well be included in the calendar, and proposes that for the future, sacrifices may be offered to her every spring and autumn. Rescript: Let the Board of Ceremonies report upon the matter."[1] Other edicts provide for the offer of incense to certain gods, the selection of lucky days for various observances, the deification of a certain maiden, etc.

Yet these curious features must not be so exaggerated as to make China appear ludicrous. The West has erred in this. China's great pretensions, her theatricalism, her hypocrisy were understood by all, and her absurdities have been allowed to fill such a place that China has been rather the laughing stock of the nations. But the Chinese are a profoundly impressive people. Nowhere else in the world has the idea of social

[1] Faber's *Famous Women of China*, p. 6.

China

or family responsibility been so developed. For example, an idiot son murders his father, and an imperial edict records that the son for such a dreadful crime has been punished by slow execution, and that the whole village has been destroyed as sharing in the offence; for had its influence been proper and properly exerted, no boy reared in the village would have committed such a crime. Nowhere else in the world has the idea of filial piety been so emphasized and honored, and it is a wonderful sight to see a whole vast Nation testifying to its real belief in immortality by the annual sacrifices to the spirits of the departed. It is true that the position of woman is subordinate and menial, and that she is valued most as the possible mother of sons. As the Book of Odes says:

> "The bears and grisly bears
> Are the auspicious intimations of sons;
> The cobras and other snakes
> Are the auspicious intimations of daughters;
> Sons shall be born to them:
> They will be put to sleep on couches;
> They will be clothed in robes;
> They will have sceptres to play with;
> Their cry will be loud.
> They will be hereafter resplendent with knee-covers,
> The future kings, the princes of the land.
> Daughters shall be born to them;
> They will be put to sleep on the ground;
> They will be clothed with wrappers;
> They will have tiles to play with.
> It will be theirs neither to do wrong nor to do good.
> Only about the spirits and the food will they have to think,
> And to cause no sorrow to their parents."[1]

---

[1] Faber's *The Status of Women in China*, p. 5.

Missions and Politics

And yet marriage has been ever regarded by the Chinese as a sacred institution, and has been carefully defended; and it may be doubted whether in any State, save the Jewish, as much has been made of the family, or it has been so truly the foundation of the State, which the Chinese call the Family of the Nation, while "prefects and magistrates are popularly styled parent officials."[1] And as to this State which has existed for forty centuries, and would exist for forty more if left to its desired seclusion, where in all history can anything more impressive be found than it, or than those great statements of its political science which Confucius framed: "If government is exercised by means of virtue, it is made as steadfast as the North pole. Mere external government (i. e. orders) is opposed to virtue. Filial piety and brotherly love are necessary; besides these two, there are no special rules. Government consists altogether in regulating, i. e. setting to right. This is achieved when the prince is prince, and the minister is minister; when the father is father, and the son is son. But the prince must desire what is good and the people will be good; therefore capital punishment is not necessary. Princes ought to go before the people.

[1] Von Möllendorff's *Family Law of the Chinese*, p. 4.

China

Then the people follow. The necessary thing is to have sufficiency of food for the people, weapons and confidence. If necessary, weapons can be dispensed with, then food, but without mutual confidence, especially of the people toward the superiors, there is no standing for the State. When those who are near are made glad then those who are far, come themselves. It should be the care of the Government to call everything by its right name, so that no wrong be secreted behind a surreptitious and hypocritical name. Good government depends chiefly upon the excellence of the prince, besides also upon qualified officials, in the election of whom the sovereign must take an interest. If the individual states, as also the imperial domain are swayed in this way, the peaceful order of the whole Empire follows as a matter of course, especially if a virtuous emperor be at the head of it."[1]

Surely it is fitting to apply to this great people the terms mighty, curious, impressive. How in the operations of Providence has such a people been produced, and for what unseen, divine purpose? There are two questions here—the question of origin and the question of destiny.

First, then, the Chinese race is what it is to-day

[1] Faber's *Systematical Digest of the Doctrines of Confucius*, pp. 94-98.

because of its isolation and its education. By her geographical position China has been separated from the whole world, as the Romans said of Britain. The mountains of Tibet rose as an insurmountable wall between China and the great wave of Western conquest which swept away the empires of Babylon and Persia, and later under the Mohammedans established itself for seven centuries in India. On the North and West stretched vast wastes of desert, untrodden and impassable, and the unploughed sea separated the Empire from all contact on the East. The Chinese language seemed yet further to isolate the Nation and to separate the people intellectually from their fellow men; while it also bound those who used it closer together. A phonetic rather than a symbolic language would have led as in Europe, to the development of different languages in different provinces or states, and so would have prevented the growth of a great Chinese race. As it is, geographical isolation shut China off from contact with languages like Sanscrit and Assyrian which would have led to modifications, and ignorant of any approximation to phonetic principles, China grew with one written and literary language, and in the main, a common spoken tongue which were

China

alike added bonds within and added barriers against those without.[1]

But isolation alone could not have produced the Chinese people. It merely provided those potential conditions in which Chinese education could have free and uninterrupted play upon the nation. As Wells Williams points out, "Their literary tendencies could never have attained the strength of an institution if they had been surrounded by more intelligent nations; nor would they have filled the land to such a degree if they had been forced to constantly defend themselves or had imbibed the lust of conquest. Either of these conditions would probably have brought their own national life to a premature close." In these literary tendencies the moral and social teachings of their great sages and rulers, their systems of education, the real kinetic energy which has fashioned and preserved the Chinese people is to be found. In the Classics compiled by Confucius all wisdom is contained, according to Chinese opinion, and the mastery of these Classics, memorizing them and learning to use their materials according to artificial and fine drawn rules, is preparation for life, training for public office and title to honor and glory. All

[1] Wells Williams' *Middle Kingdom*, Vol. ii., pp. 188-190.

preferment is based on success in the Government examinations in the knowledge and use of the Classics. Some Chinese historians maintain that appointment to office was first conditioned on competitive examinations by the Emperor Shun in the year 2200 B. C. Though this may be doubted, it is certain that now the system penetrates the whole Empire, and thousands and hundreds of thousands, even millions compete for the degrees, the lowest, or "Budding Genius" corresponding rudely to our B. A., the second, "Promoted Scholar" a sort of M. A., the third, "Fit for Office," a sort of D. C. L., or LL. D. To which may be added a fourth, or "Hanlin" degree, by which the successful scholar becomes a member of the Hanlin Academy or "Forest of Pencils." About one per cent. of the rough scholars get the degree of "Budding Genius," and from the fact that 25,000 with this degree will compete at one provincial capital for the second degree, one gains some idea of the number of candidates. About one per cent. of the "Budding Geniuses" become "Fit for Office."[1]

The subjects of these examinations for centuries have of course furnished the staple of

[1] Martin's *The Chinese*, pp. 39-84.

China

thought of the Chinese people, and the Classics have thus been woven into the very grain and texture of the Chinese race. They have memorized them and the commentaries upon them and have looked upon their absorption and the modelling of life upon them, as the consummation of all duties. How thoroughly they have been expected to do this such questions as these from the examination papers will indicate: "How do the rival schools of Wang and Ching differ in respect to the exposition of the meaning and the criticism of the Book of Changes?" "The art of war arose under Hwang te, forty-four hundred years ago. Different dynasties have since that time adopted different regulations in regard to the use of militia or standing armies, the mode of raising supplies for the army, etc. Can you state these briefly?" Or, note such a subject for an essay as this passage from the Analects of Confucius. "Confucius said, 'How majestic was the manner in which Shun and Yu held possession of the Empire, as if it were nothing to them.' Confucius said, 'Great indeed was Yaou as a sovereign! How majestic was he! It is only Heaven that is grand and only Yaou corresponded to it! How vast was his virtue! The people could find no name for it.'" A few years ago the University of London admitted to its initial examinations annually about 1,400 candidates, and passed one-half. The Government examinations of China at the same time admitted about 2,000,000 annually, and passed one per cent.[1]

This great device has worked for centuries now. As Dr. Martin has pointed out, "It has served the State as a safety valve, providing a career for those ambitious spirits which might otherwise foment disturbances or excite revolutions. It operates as a counterpoise to the power of an absolute monarch. With it a man of talent may raise himself from the humblest ranks to the dignity of viceroy or premier. It gives the Government a hold on the educated gentry, and binds them to the support of existing institutions." And its influence on the character and opinion of the people has been simply enormous. That "the Chinese may be regarded as the only pagan nation which has maintained democratic habits under a purely despotic theory of Government; that this Government has respected the rights of its subjects by placing them under the protection of law, with its sanctions and tribunals (and keeping them there) and making the sovereign

[1] Idem, pp. 51, 52.

China

amenable in the popular mind for the continuance of his sway to the approval of a higher Power able to punish him; that it has prevented the domination of all feudal, hereditary and priestly classes and interests by making the tenure of officers of Government below the throne chiefly depend on their literary attainments;"—all this is due to the influence of their educational system and the body of teaching it has ground into the Nation.[1]

On the other hand, the weaknesses and inefficiencies of China to-day are in great measure directly traceable to the same influence and teaching. The literati, "the most influential portion of the population," are the most conservative, bigoted and narrow-minded. "The Chinese have drawn their self-conceit and contempt for all foreigners as barbarians from the ancient works." "The scholar of the first degree," says their proverb, "without going abroad is able to know what transpires under the whole heaven." Confucius lived six centuries before Christ. To make what he knew and the wisdom of those who went before him the total of all available wisdom and to school men into this conviction until it is ineradicable has been one result of the

[1] Wells Williams' *Middle Kingdom*, Vol. ii., p. 191.

Missions and Politics

Chinese system of education. It has limited knowledge and life to the level of the far past, and has made fidelity to this old antediluvianism the test of all things. Chinese education has isolated China in time as it was of old isolated by language and in space. Confucianism has shown itself as stereotyped and sterile as Islam.

This is not an uncharitable judgment. History and the present evidence of life have passed it. Confucianism has limited the horizon of men to the wisdom of twenty-five centuries ago. "The past is made for slaves," said Emerson, and whatever truth is in his saying applies to the Chinese. Confucianism recognizes no relation to a living God. It relegates all contact with Heaven even to an annual act of the Emperor. It ignores the plainest facts of moral character. It has no serious idea of sin, and indeed no deeper insight at all. It cannot explain death. It holds truth of light account. It presupposes and tolerates polygamy and sanctions polytheism. It confounds ethics with external ceremonies and reduces social life to tyranny. It rises at the highest no higher than the worship of genius, the deification of man.[1]

Indeed the Chinese themselves long ago passed

[1] Faber's *Systematical Digest of the Doctrine of Confucius*, pp. 124-131.

China

judgment upon the inadequacy of Confucianism, and with that utter disregard of logical consistency which is another of their inexplicable divergences from the ways of the West, added to their Confucian beliefs the most un-Confucian ideas of Taoism and Buddhism. The Chinese have never been capable, however, of holding either of these religions in even an approximately pure form. Taoism was in Lao Tse's hands a high transcendental idealism, but his followers reduced it to alchemy and necromancy. Buddhism was a sort of atheistic mysticism, but in China it became a system of magic or spiritual thaumaturgy. Any line of division between these two became obscured, and both were absorbed by the Chinese to supply in a measure those spiritual longings which Confucianism had been futile to suppress, and to which it had no ministry. But Taoism and Buddhism while having firm hold upon the Nation, and tinging the life of every man, supplying those elements of superstition and real religion which the agnosticism of Confucianism ignored, have never been able to shake the older system, and have not modified in the direction of enlightenment and broader sympathy the education of the Chinese race. Isolated at the beginning, twenty-five centuries of narrowing discipline have separated the Chinese by a mighty chasm from other Nations and the sweep of human progress, holding them

> "Aloof from our mutations and unrest
> Alien to our achievements and desires."

It is not at all strange that people of such a character and education should have assumed toward the rest of the world the attitude they have. Before the Western Nations molested them, their Empire was the mistress of all. The little kingdoms round about she treated with patronage or contempt. When the Western Nations came, she judged them by her dependent tribes, and spoke to them as she had spoken to her tributary neighbors. "She assumed a tone of superiority, pronounced them barbarians and demanded tribute." This was due to her ignorance and conceit. Her conceit abides, and it is to be feared, so also does her ignorance. Thus the author of *China's Intercourse with Europe* wherein the facts are given from the Chinese point of view, says, "As for the petty States of the German Zollverein . . . many of them are unknown even by name in the historical and geographical works accessible to us, and we have no means of establishing the fact of their alleged existence!"[1] A

[1] *China's Intercourse with Europe*, p. 114.

China

correspondent of the London *Times* recently told of a conversation with some Chinese officials on the Tibetan border, in which reference was made to the capture of Peking in 1862 by the French and English. "Yes," said the officials laughing, "we know you said you went there, and we read with much amusement your gazettes giving your account of it all. They were very cleverly written and we dare say deceived your own subjects into a belief that you actually went to Peking. We often do the same thing."[1] And even in the famous memorial which was presented in 1895, signed by 1,300 scholars who had taken the second degree and represented fourteen out of the Eighteen Provinces of China, and which urged a number of reforms, the establishment of banks and post offices, railways, encouragement of machinery, mining, newspapers, education, etc., the following sentences occur, showing the most naïve ignorance of the world. "Let the most advanced students of Confucianism be called up by the Emperor to the capital and given the Hanlin degree and funds to go abroad. If they succeed in establishing schools in foreign countries where are gathered 1,000 pupils, let them be ennobled. Thus we shall take

[1] Norman's *Peoples and Politics of the Far East*, p. 286.

Missions and Politics

Confucianism and with it civilize all the barbarians, and under the cloak of preaching Confucianism, travel abroad and quickly learn the motives of the barbarians and extend the fame of our country."

These words of the 1,300 scholars indicate another element of China's training and of the present situation. Not only are the Chinese a mighty, curious and impressive people whom Western Nations have misunderstood and despised, but the Chinese have also misunderstood as well as despised the Western peoples. Those same features of their character and education which make them so unintelligible to us make us unintelligible to them. The memorial of the 1,300 scholars proposes that Confucian missionaries be sent both to civilize the barbarians of the West, and to learn just what our motives are. From the Chinese point of view, these seem to me to be eminently just and reasonable propositions. And even from an unbiased and intermediate point of view it must be acknowledged that a candid comparison of Western and Chinese civilizations does not leave everything to be said on one side. With a pure Christian civilization Confucian civilization could not stand comparison for a moment, but it can have its own word to

China

say in any controversy with our actual present stage of civilization in the West. And as to Chinese confusion as to the real motives of Western Nations, who can wonder that they are an enigma to the Chinese? Are they not to us? Who can disentangle the sincere from the selfish and false? "Your code of morals is defective in one point," said Li Hung Chang once, "it lays too much stress on charity and too little on justice." Who can reconcile the professed motives of the Mission movement with the obvious purposes of European Governments? We know they are irreconcilable and do not try, but they are the double face of a single party to the Chinese. Besides he cannot understand the restlessness of the West, its unwillingness to stay at home, its constant spirit of disturbance, of change, the lust of innovation, its domineering impetuousness, its obtrusiveness, its irritating refusal to let China alone. Nor could we understand these things if we were in the place of the Chinese. Indeed even in our own place much of our spirit and of the spirit of our Western peoples is unintelligible to us, save as the inherited genius of the race, and much of it as displayed in dealings with Oriental Nations from Turkey to China is as a foul stench in our nostrils.

Missions and Politics

Here then have been all the elements of a most interesting situation which has altered but slightly since the gates of China were forced about fifty years ago. On one side a Nation numbering one-fourth of the human race, not comprehending, heartily despising the Western Nations, desiring to be let alone and to live on in the ancient ways of the sages. On the other, the forceful Nations of the West not comprehending China, viewing her ludicrously and with contempt, but insisting on intercourse, on equal terms, and demanding that China should forego her desire for seclusion and open to the world. This struggle and the forces which have entered into it, have constituted the last of the influences which have produced the China of our present history, until within the last few months the European Nations have threatened the integrity of the Eighteen Provinces. The want of proportion in our historical knowledge is in nothing more clearly shown than in our ignorance of the steps in this great struggle, especially of the real character and meaning of the Opium and Arrow Wars. The average student knows only, as the current oratory runs: "that Great Britain forced opium on helpless and protesting China at the mouth of her cannon," and scarcely stops to think of the deeper significance

China

of those acts in the great movement which had to do with the welfare and destiny of one-fourth of the human race, yes and the welfare and destiny of perhaps two-fourths more. The first war, 1839-1842, opened the five treaty ports of Canton, Amoy, Foochow, Ningpo and Shanghai, ceded Hong Kong to Great Britain, authorized trade and recognized foreigners. "Looked at in any point of view," says the most solid writer on China, "political, commercial, moral or intellectual, it will always be considered as one of the turning points in the history of mankind, involving the welfare of all nations in its wide-reaching consequences. . . . It was extraordinary in its origin, as growing chiefly out of a commercial misunderstanding; remarkable in its course as being waged between strength and weakness, conscious superiority and ignorant pride; melancholy in its end as forcing the weaker to pay for the opium within its borders against all its laws, thus paralyzing the little moral power its feeble Government could exert to protect its subjects; and momentous in its results as introducing, on a basis of acknowledged obligations, one-half of the world to the other, without any arrogant demands from the victors, or humiliating concessions from the vanquished. It was a turning-point in the national life of the

Missions and Politics

Chinese race."[1] The second war, 1857-1860, grew out of an occurrence of a most trivial character, and was marked by the pursuit of the most petty, private and even unjustifiable ends;[2] but it resulted in the opening of nine more treaty ports; it conceded the right to travel throughout the Eighteen Provinces, and contained a special clause giving protection to foreigners and natives in the propagation and adoption of the Christian religion.

Now although troubles over opium were the occasion of the first war, the real issues were general trade intercourse and reciprocal and equal diplomatic relations as necessary thereto. "The merchants of Great Britain," said Lord Napier before the war, "wish to trade with all China on principles of mutual benefit; they will never relax their exertions till they gain a point of equal importance to both countries, and the viceroy will find it as easy to stop the current of the Canton River as to carry into effect the insane determinations of the Hong," (to resist these trade advances). Opium was an accident and not an essential of the wars. As a Chinese writer has said in a novel account of this matter, "It is plain that it

---
[1] Wells Williams' *Middle Kingdom*, Vol. ii., pp. 463, 464.
[2] Martin's *A Cycle of Cathay*, pp. 143-190.

China

was not the destruction of the opium, but the stoppage of trade, which caused these wars. . . . This was sufficient to disappoint and provoke men who had come thousands of miles for the sake of gain. . . . Worms only appear in a rotten carcase, and it was only when exaction followed exaction and justice was denied to creditors, that the foreigners turned upon us. War would have followed all the same even if the opium trade had been stopped; and in fact opium only came because profits being impossible by fair, the foreigners were driven to obtain them by foul means. Some people argue that it was the granting of trade in the first instance that brought on our troubles. But this is absurd; for China can do without foreigners, whilst foreigners are dependent upon us for tea and rhubarb, and therefore are at our mercy. All that is wanted is fair trade to secure their willing loyalty."[1] But it was not trade only. It was also the recognition of equality and respect that the Western Nations demanded. This the Chinese officials had contemptuously refused. "The great ministers of the Chinese Empire . . . are not permitted to have intercourse with outside bar-

---

[1] Parker's *Chinese Account of the Opium War*, and *China's Intercourse with Europe*, p. 55.

Missions and Politics

barians," said the Viceroy of Canton to the English Envoy. In reporting the matter to Peking, the Canton Governor said, "On the face of the envelope (which the barbarian Envoy presented) the forms and style of equality were used, and there were absurdly written the characters 'Great English Nation.' Now it is plain on the least reflection, that in keeping the central and outside people apart, it is of the highest importance to maintain dignity and sovereignty. Whether the said barbarian has or has not official rank there are no means of thoroughly ascertaining. But though he be really an officer of the said Nation, he yet cannot write letters on equality with frontier officers of the Celestial Empire." Later the Governor issued a paper deprecating the disturbance of trade and saying, "Lord Napier's previous opposition necessarily demands such a mode of procedure, and it would be most right immediately to put a stop to buying and selling. But considering that the said Nation's King has hitherto been in the highest degree reverently obedient, he cannot in sending Lord Napier at this time have desired him thus obstinately to resist. The some hundreds of thousands of commercial duties yearly coming from the said country concern not the Celestial Empire the extent of a hair or a feather's down. . . . But the tea, the rhubarb, the raw silk of the Inner Land, are the sources by which England's people live and maintain life. For the fault of one man, Lord Napier, must the livelihood of the whole Nation be precipitately cut off? . . . I cannot bring my mind to bear it."[1] And this tone of contempt and insult continued without exception or relief. What could Western Nations do in the face of it? They could quietly go home and abandon trade with China save on terms of inferiority. China wondered that they so persistently refused to do this. But the passion for trade, and the trade God who rules the diplomacy of nations was fiercer even in Western Nations than among the Chinese. They would trade, and they would trade on terms of self-respect, and to accomplish that in this century could only be done by war, and war that meant to China disgrace, the withdrawal of insult, the abandonment of her traditional attitude and the destruction of her isolated seclusion, and that could only leave with her ruling class the sting of defeat, the sense of doom and a bitter hatred of that restless, encroaching force that tears men away from the slavery of the past and thrusts

[1] Wells Williams' *Middle Kingdom*, Vol. ii., pp. 468, 472.

Missions and Politics

them out into the future, like Abraham, not knowing whither they go.

This roughly is the general situation, and so much of history has been set forth in it because in China every present situation contains the past as its chief element. What is to grow out of this situation? Whither is God leading the Chinese? Is their day spent, their history done, or is there yet hope for them?

First, there is no hope for them in Confucianism. It has had free scope for twenty-five centuries, and while it has accomplished the results that have been recognized, it contains absolutely no hope for the future. Progress is impossible under it. It ties the race hand and foot and flings it back into a patriarchal dotage. As to Buddhism, while its superstitions and idols supply what they can to meet the irrepressible spiritual needs of the people, its priests, as Eitel says, "Are mostly recruited from the lowest classes, and one finds among them frequently the most wretched specimens of humanity, more devoted to opium smoking than any other class in China. They have no intellectual tastes, they have centuries ago ceased to cultivate the study of Sanscrit, they know next to nothing about the history of their own religion, living together mostly in idleness, and occasionally going out to earn some money by reading litanies for the dead, or acting as exorcists and sorcerers or physicians. No community of interest, no ties of social life, no object of generous ambition, beyond the satisfying of those wants which bind them to the cloister, diversify the monotonous current of their daily life," while "the people as a whole have no respect for the Buddhist Church and habitually sneer at the Buddhist priests."[1] As for Taoism the high and noble views of Lao Tse have sunk to the lowest oracularism, and its superstitions are only a grade below those of Buddhism with which now in China it is inextricably interwoven. The most pitiably abject human being I ever saw was a Taoist priest, with long matted hair run through with straws, half naked, begging in the streets of Peking. In her own religions, there is no hope for China.

Nor is there any in her political and civil institutions. They are rotten through and through, though sufficient for her old life and isolation, but she is not allowed her old life and isolation any longer. The introduction of mathematics and Western sciences and even questions as to the Bible into the competitive examinations, the throb of the railway past the graves of the

[1] Eitel's *Buddhism*, pp. 33, 34.

Missions and Politics

sages, the profile of the telegraph against the dragon outline of the hills, the hum of the spindle in the cotton mills, and engines in the silk factories, and the ramifying filaments of Western trade introduce conditions for which the old forms and the old officials are unfit. It will be enough if they can keep up with the new times. There is no leading in them.

And although we believe that God is in His heaven and all's well with His world, and that the conduct of European nations in China at the present time will in the end work into His mighty purposes, and indeed is working into those purposes even now, this seems to me a disheartening quarter to which to turn for help and hope. Mr. Curzon may entertain the curious fancy of a secular redemption. "The best hope of salvation for the old and moribund in Asia, the wisest lessons for the emancipated and new, are still to be derived from the ascendency of British character, and under the shelter, where so required, of British dominion."[1] But where is the redemptive power that has regenerated Hong Kong and Singapore? And how much salvation has come to Shanghai from Foochow Road? Has French rule brought hope to Tonquin? Has Spain given

[1] Curzon's *Problems of the Far East*, new ed., p. 15.

China

help to the Philippines? Wherein has Borneo been redeemed by the Dutch or Bokhara by the Russians? If the real partition of China comes, as it may, and Russia takes Manchuria and Chili, and Germany Shantung, and England the valleys of the Yangtse and the West Rivers, and the whole body and heart of China lying between, and France Hainan and the southern section of Kwangtung and Kwang Si and Yunnan,[1]—it will mean good I am sure, though what an ignominious end of the Middle and Heavenly Kingdom it will be!—but it is not the direction in which one turns for help or hope, especially with the sounds of trade so filling the air, the clamor of the navies and the shouts of Prince Henry preaching the gospel of the consecrated person of the queer Emperor of Germany, and William's Minister of Foreign Affairs saying in the *Reichstag* "that Germany could no longer exclude herself from sharing the promising new markets. That the time had passed when Germany was content to look on and see other countries dividing the world among them, while Germany contented herself with a place in heaven. The intentions of Germany toward China were benevolent . . . but Germany could not permit China to treat

[1] Martin's *Cycle of Cathay*, p. 399.

German interests as subordinate to those of other nations." And the speaker concluded, the cable dispatch said, "amid long and loud applause by saying 'We will not put other people in the shade, but we claim for ourselves a place in the sun.'" That was a pertinent prayer of the Queen's Jubilee:—

> "If drunk with sight of power we loose
> Wild tongues that have not Thee in awe—
> Such boastings as the Gentiles use
> Or lesser breeds without the Law—
> Lord God of Hosts, be with us yet,
> Lest we forget—lest we forget.
>
> "For heathen heart that puts her trust
> In reeking tube and iron shard—
> All valiant dust that builds on dust,
> And guarding calls not Thee to guard—
> For frantic boast and foolish word,
> Thy mercy on Thy people, Lord."

Yet it must be admitted that the tumult of the Captains and the Kings seems to the people to be the force supreme. And it may make very visible changes on the maps and create new names for the histories and for a generation seem to be controlling character and life, but the long view of history and the deeper insight will lead us to look further still for any permanent source of help and hope for China. For those forces are the greatest which most affect character. Confucianism is so powerful and so hopeless because of its enormous influence upon the character of

China

the people. Determinations of territorial boundaries and assignments of political authority are minor and insignificant in comparison with the forces which run down to the roots of personal life. And of these forces time will show that none is running deeper or spreading more widely than Christianity.

Christianity was first brought to China by the Nestorians early in the sixth century, and the only known traces of their work are preserved in the famous Nestorian tablet found in the Province of Shansi in 1725. The Roman Catholics began their work in the thirteenth century, and with glorious devotion, and some readiness to temporize, to flatter, to dissemble and to deceive. Their work grew greatly, winning at last the favor of the Emperor Kanghi until Clement XI. joined issue with him over ancestral worship and some other ceremonies, and then the missionaries were expelled from the country. From 1767 to 1820 they were persecuted, ordered to leave or slain, but continued apparently to conduct themselves in the manner of which one of their own number, Pere Repa complained, saying, "If our European missionaries in China would conduct themselves with less ostentation[1] and accommo-

[1] Vid. also Monseigneur Reynoud's *Another China*, p. 39, which is a Roman Catholic view.

Missions and Politics

date their manners to persons of all ranks and conditions, the number of converts would be immensely increased. Their garments are made of the richest materials . . . and as they never mix with the people, they make but few converts." As a matter of fact, however, they have made many converts and doubtless many good Christians. Protestant Missions began with Morrison in 1807, and together with Roman Catholic Missions were recognized and legalized by the treaties made after the war of 1860. Article VIII. of the British treaty reads " The Christian religion as professed by Protestants or Roman Catholics inculcates the practice of virtue and teaches men to do as they would be done by. Persons teaching it or professing it, therefore, shall alike be entitled to the protection of the Chinese authorities; nor shall any such, peaceably pursuing their calling, and not offending against the laws, be persecuted or interfered with."

Thus introduced and recognized two things have prevented Christianity's exercise of its full power One has been the difficulty of adjusting it to the Chinese mind in such a way as not to commit it to anything unessential which is repugnant to the Chinese mind, and to fit it precisely to the fundamental spiritual needs and ca-

China

pacities of the race. I asked one of the ablest missionaries in China, what were the great problems of the work in China, and he replied instantly, "They are one—How to present Christ to the Chinese mind." There is nothing else on earth like that mind, so full of distortions, of atrophies, of abnormalities, of curious twists and deficiencies, and how to avoid all unnecessary prejudice and difficulty, and to make use of prepared capacity and notion so as to gain for the Christian message the most open and unbiased reception, is a problem unsolved as yet and beyond any of our academic questionings here. For example, the Chinese idea of filial piety has in it much that is Christian and noble and true, and yet much that is absurd and untrue. To recognize and avail of the former aspects and not to alienate and anger in stripping off the latter, is one phase of this problem. Where is there one more wonderfully interesting and more baffling?

The second thing that has hampered Christianity has been its political entanglements. The last few months have given a characteristic illustration of this. The murder of two German missionaries in Shantung province was at once made the pretext of seizing a bay with its protecting fortifications, and bade fair to precipitate

Missions and Politics

the dismemberment of the Chinese Empire. Is it wonderful that the Chinese distrust the character of the Mission movement, are sceptical as to its non-political character, and view Christianity with suspicion? China has disliked the Western Nations from the start. Their overbearing willfulness, their remorseless aggression, their humiliating victories, their very peccable diplomacy have all strengthened her dislike. The unfortunate occasion of the first war which brought Great Britain forward as the defender of the wretched opium traffic, which the Chinese Central Government at least was making sincere efforts to suppress, placed the Western Nations in the position of supporting by arms what China knew to be morally wrong. The general bearing of the foreign commercial class, ignorant of the language, of the people and of their prejudices has increased the anti-foreign feeling of the Chinese yet more. The charge that the missionary movement as a religious movement is responsible for the anti-foreign feeling is fantastic and it is not supported by facts. Missions have made a hundred friends to every foe.

The missionary would undoubtedly in any event have had to share some of this hatred, as a member of one of the objectionable na-

China

tionalities; but the Chinese are capable of distinctions, and would soon have learned that the Mission movement was sharply distinct from all political bearings, if indeed it had been so. But from the beginning of foreign intercourse, the trader and the missionary have been classed together. The same rights have been claimed for each, and the claim was enforced by war in the case of the trader, and the consequent treaties included the missionary. Ever since, through the legations, missionary rights under the treaties have perhaps been the chief matter of business, and outrages on missionaries have been followed by demands for reparation and indemnity. No Government was willing to surrender its duty to protect its citizens, and even if the missionaries had refused protection, it would have been forced on them for the sake of maintaining traditional prestige, and defending traders and trade interests from assault.

In consequence, the missionary work has been unable to appear as the propaganda of a kingdom that is not of this world. The Chinese officials are unable, with few exceptions, to conceive of it except as a part of the political scheme of Western Nations to acquire influence in China, and to subvert the Government and the principles

Missions and Politics

of loyalty on which it rests. "It is our opinion that foreign missionaries are in very truth the source whence springs all trouble in China," so says one of the Chinese "Blue Books." "Foreigners come to China from a distance of several ten thousands of miles, and from about ten different countries with only two objects in view; namely, trade and religious propagandism. With the former they intend to gradually deprive China of her wealth, and with the latter they likewise seek to steal away the hearts of her people. The ostensible pretext they put forward is, the cultivation of friendly relations: what their hidden purpose is, is unfathomable."[1] Even a Roman Catholic priest, and his people are the worst offenders in this, writes: "Whence comes this obstinate determination to reject Christianity? It is not religious fanaticism, for no people are so far gone as the Chinese in scepticism and indifference. One may be a disciple of Confucius or of Lao Tse, Mussulman or Buddhist, the Chinese Government does not regard it. It is only against the Christian religion it seeks to defend itself. It sees all Europe following on the heels of the Apostles of Christ, Europe with her ideas, her civilization, and with *that* it will have absolutely

[1] Michie's *China and Christianity*, p. 101.

China

nothing to do, being rightly or wrongly satisfied with the ways of its fathers."[1]

Out of a very profound ignorance of the subject of Missions in China, Mr. Henry Norman, after alluding to "the minute results of good and the considerable results of harm" they produce, says, "At any rate, in considering the future of China, the missionary influence cannot be counted upon for any good."[2] I believe that its affiliations with the political and commercial schemes of the West, which are Mr. Norman's deities, and the way France and Germany make it a cat's-paw are seriously hindering it from doing its purely spiritual work; but even with this hindrance and the difficulty of a wise adjustment to the Chinese mind, with its aptitudes and incapacities, it is the most penetrating and permeating force working in China to lead her on to the new day, and its messengers are the heralds of the dawn. "Believe nobody when he sneers at them," said Colonel Denby. "The man is simply not posted." The 1,300 scholars, whose memorial I have already quoted, know better than to sneer. "Every province is full of chapels," they wrote, "whilst we have only one temple in each county

---

[1] Michie's *Missionaries in China*, p. 67.
[2] Norman's *Peoples and Politics of the Far East*, pp. 280-282, 304-308.

Missions and Politics

for our sage Confucius. Is this not painful? Let religious instruction be given in each county. Let all the charitable institutions help. Let all the unowned temples and charity guilds be made into temples of the Confucian religion, and thus make the people good, and stop the progress of strange doctrines." When Bishop Moule, who is still living at Hangchow, came to China, there were only forty Protestants in the Empire. Now there are 80,000, and in addition the multitudes enrolled in the Church of Rome. They are erring who are not reckoning with the powerful work the Christian Church is doing amid the foundations of the Chinese Empire. She blows few trumpets from the housetops. She boasts with no naval displays. Her trust is not put in reeking tube and iron shard. Guarding she calls on God to guard, and under His guarding is doing at the roots of Chinese life the work of the new creation, and out of her work a Church is rising of a new sort. It will have its own heresies and trials, but it will have elements of power which have belonged to none of God's other peoples; and I think it will lean back on the rock of the rule of the Living God which we are abandoning for the rule of our own wills. And whether the Chinese race shall serve the future as one nation or as the peaceful and submissive fragments of a once mighty Empire, this much is true:—the service they will render will have been touched by Christ whose movement will go on "until all the cities, towns, villages and hamlets of that vast Empire have the teacher and professor of religion living in them, until their children are taught, their liberties understood, their rights assured, their poor cared for, their literature purified, and their condition bettered in this world by the full revelation of another made known to them,"[1] out of which One has come greater than Confucius, greater than Lao Tse, to dwell among men and be their Living King.

[1] Wells Williams' *Middle Kingdom*, Vol. ii., p. 371.

LECTURE IV

Japan

My soul is sailing through the sea,
But the Past is heavy and hindereth me.
The Past hath crusted cumbrous shells
That hold the flesh of cold sea-mells
      About my soul.
The huge waves wash, the high waves roll
Each barnacle clingeth and worketh dole
  And hindereth me from sailing!

Old Past let go, and drop i' the sea
Till fathomless waters cover thee!
For I am living but thou art dead;
Thou drawest back, I strive ahead
      The Day to find.
Thy shells unbind! Night comes behind,
I needs must hurry with the wind,
  And trim me best for sailing.

                SYDNEY LANIER, *Barnacles.*

LECTURE IV

JAPAN

"IT is like passing from night into day," says Mr. Chirrol, in *The Far Eastern Question*, expressing the common feeling of travellers, "from an atmosphere laden with the oppressive odors of decay into one charged with the ozone of exuberant vitality. On the Western shores of the Yellow Sea the traveller has left behind him a countless conglomeration of human beings which no homogeneity of race, language or religion has availed to weld together into a nation, a cumbersome and corrupt bureaucracy which barely continues to keep the ponderous machinery of Government moving in the well-worn ruts of time-honored abuses, and a central authority, loose and shiftless at the best, and now distracted to the verge of utter hopelessness and imbecility. On its Eastern shores he lands amongst a people whose national vigor has been strung to the highest point of tension by a strenuously centralized administration which itself responds in complete sympathy of intellect and heart to the touch of enlightened and resolute rulers. Alone amongst all Asiatic Nations, Japan seems to have realized in its fullest sense the modern conception of patriotism, such as we understand it in the West. In China the eyes of even the best among the living generation are hypnotized by constant contemplation of the dead past; in Japan all eyes are straining toward the future. On the one hand the chaos of misrule, corruption and ignorance; on the other, a rigid discipline based on an individual sense of duty and an innate love of order. In China an almost universal trend downward into the common slough of despond; in Japan a combined effort to level upward. In both countries the lower classes are patient and industrious; but while in China what remains to them of the fruits of their industry after they have been squeezed by their rulers, is too often squandered in opium smoking, and in an insensate mania for gambling, thrift is the rule in Japan. In both countries they are easily governed, but in China there is the dull, unreasoning resignation of the overworked beast of burden, in Japan the ready acquiescence of a bright and light-hearted people instinct with the joyousness of life."

This bright antithesis is not wholly just, but it serves well to emphasize the fact that China and

Japan

Japan have chosen different paths even as they are marked by radically different racial temperaments. Their temperaments have differed from the beginning. They chose the divergent paths fifty years ago. Until then, the period of the Opium War in China and of Commodore Perry's visit to Japan, the two Empires held the same attitude toward the outside world. Since then they have separated from one another as the East from the West. "China compelled to abandon her old exclusiveness has yielded as little as possible," and is bogged still deep in the mire of Confucian antiquity and unprogressiveness. Japan renounced her isolation without waiting for the application of force and has launched out into a new life, having a place now at the council board of the Nations. There is scarcely a better illustration in history of "the immense advantage which an active striving for the better possesses over an inert adherence to tradition."

From the third century B. C., when the builder of the great wall, though failing to subject Japan, still brought her in a measure under the intellectual influence of China, until the dividing of the ways between the two Nations in our own century, China and Japan have stood together in history and in the minds of the Western Nations as pre-

Missions and Politics

serving in the main a policy of seclusion and aloofness. Of their own history during the earlier centuries, the Japanese themselves know little. There are no reliable records of the period prior to the fifth century of our era. When authentic history begins we see a people whose origin is unknown, possessing evident gifts of adaptation, developing an interesting political system, and absorbing civilization and arts from neighboring Continental lands. This tide poured in through Korea in the period between the third and eighth centuries. It brought with it Chinese philosophy, Confucian morals and Chinese literature. Tailors, excellent horses, annalists, mulberry trees, silk worms, architects, diviners, astronomers, doctors, mathematicians, learned men came over from Korea, and by no means least of all, those secrets of ceramics which were long ago lost in the land of their origin but which have made Japanese pottery famous.

The Japanese readily acknowledge these obligations and draw their own conclusions from their successful absorption of Chinese and Korean civilization. As one of them writes in a recent article, "In spite of the readiness and energy we have shown in our reforms and general progress, it has been doubted whether we could

Japan

really assimilate the civilization of the West. . . . But one who has taken the trouble to study the history of our Nation cannot fail to see that she was singularly prepared to receive the light from the West. Formerly, Japan adopted ideas and institutions from the Continent of Asia, infused them with a spirit peculiar to her people, and developed them according to the needs of her situation, even after these ideas and institutions had degenerated or even disappeared in the land of their origin. <u>It was Confucianism which formed the foundation of the Japanese ethical conceptions.</u> Our social institutions were also largely borrowed from China. Even Buddhism, which has made the nations of continental Asia mild and sluggish, exercised in Japan a healthy influence. . . . Generally speaking," he adds, "the statement that life consists in receiving from without and assimilating within seems to apply to no form of life with greater truth than to the life of Japan."[1]

As the writer I have just quoted intimates, more was borrowed than just Confucian literature and Chinese civilization. The great missionary religion which had died away in India, only to come to mightier life in lands to the East

[1] *The Far East*, English Edition of *Kokumin-no-Tomo*, Vol. i., No. 1, p.9.

Missions and Politics

and North, came in also.[1] In the sixth century, the Korean rulers presented a number of Buddhist books, idols, etc., to several Mikados, and the new faith made way, but slowly, though some members of the royal family accepted it and so made it the fashionable thing to be priests or nuns. Seventy-five years after its introduction there were but forty-six temples in the land. After twenty-five years of Protestant Missions there were ten times as many Christian churches. But it was in the eighth century under the Emperor Shomu, who spoke of himself as "the servant of Buddha, the Law and the Priesthood," and who commanded that two temples should be built in each province, that the new religion took deep root working its way down among the lower classes, one of the few illustrations in history of a religion's acceptance first by the rich and the great and its subsequent adaptation to the poor, although, as Dr. Gordon of Kioto has pointed out, even with the perpetration of "the most gigantic of pious frauds in its propagation, it took many centuries for it to reach the popular heart, and it never gained that undivided allegiance which we regard as a *sine qua non* to the faith of the Christian."[2]

[1] *Transactions of the Asiatic Society of Japan*, Vol. xiv., Part I., pp. 73-80.
[2] *Proceedings of the Osaka Conference*, 1883, p. 92.

Japan

With all these borrowings, however, the Japanese did develop two original things: a dual system of government, and an interesting Oriental feudalism. In the twelfth century, Yoritomo established the former, the Mikado appointing him Shogun in 1192, and so initiating the system which was abolished in 1868, when the Mikado came out of his divine retirement and took back from the Shoguns the power which for seven centuries they had administered in his name and with the sanctions of his heavenly origin and authority. Feudalism grew out of the Shogunate by three steps—the first when Yoritomo obtained full military authority as High Constable of the realm, and appointed military magistrates throughout the provinces; the second when the Ashikoga Shoguns made the magistracies hereditary in the families of their own nominees; the third when the Shogun Hideyoshi parcelled out the fiefs by titles in his own name without reference to the sovereign, and when Iyeyasu based the power of his dynasty on the tie of personal fealty to himself and his successors as lords paramount of the lands of the daimios and hatamatos.[1]

---

[1] *The Japan Mail*, Nov. 25, 1876, quoted in Griffis's *The Mikado's Empire*, p. 228.

Missions and Politics

During these centuries of isolation from the West life moved slowly in Japan. The absorption of Chinese civilization and its modifications under Japanese feudalism were not enlivening processes. During a period of 120 years under the last line of the Shoguns the population of the land increased less than in any two years since 1886.

There was, however, one period in these centuries when the life of the West touched Japan and then was cast out while the gates were shut more securely than in all the ages before. In the sixteenth century, Portuguese trading vessels began to visit Japan, where they exchanged Western commodities for the products, then little known, of the Japanese Islands. The Dutch and the English followed the Portuguese. The visitors gained a good foothold; trade prospered and the Roman Catholic missionaries both at Kioto and throughout the country enrolled many converts. As long as the papal order confining the privilege of evangelizing Japan to the Jesuits was obeyed, things went favorably on the whole, but soon some Spanish Franciscans came from the Philippines and jealousies and suspicious representations added to the indiscreet statements of a Spanish pilot as to the political objects of the

Japan

Jesuits and other missionaries aroused the anger of the Japanese, one of whose historians declares, the missionaries' "plan of action was to tend the sick and relieve the poor, and so prepare the way for the reception of Christianity, and then to convert every one, and to make the sixty-six provinces of Japan subject to Portugal." This suspicion of Christianity was doubtless confirmed by "the course of events in China, the jealousy of the native priests, the control of their converts exercised by the missionaries, the connection of Christianity with trade and the astounding progress made by it in the space of half a century."[1] And in 1613 the edict of expulsion was issued, the tragedy of Shimabara closing the history in 1637, and 30,000 Christians baptizing in blood the new era of revived nationalism and exclusiveness.

Two centuries after this, Perry appeared in the Bay of Yeddo, and the old days were gone forever. Within Japan forces had been at work preparing the land for the new age. There was restlessness against the Tokugawa Shogun's exclusivism, and four distinct movements were under way striving to effect, first "the overthrow of the Shogun and his reduction to his

[1] *Transactions of the Asiatic Society of Japan*, Vol. vi., No. 1, p. 21.

proper level as a vassal; second, the restoration of the true Emperor to supreme power; third, the abolition of the feudal system and a return to the ancient imperial regime; fourth, the abolition of Buddhism and the establishment of pure Shinto as the national faith and the engine of government."[1] But while in the minds of some, these ends were combined with a policy of advocating the abandonment of exclusiveness, the adoption of Western civilization, and the entrance of Japan into the comity of nations, in the minds of others they were associated with an intense dislike of foreigners, the expulsion of barbarians and the perpetual isolation of Japan from the rest of the world. But whatever the opinions of men were with reference to foreign intercourse, they were agreed in condemning the professions of sovereignty put forth by the Shogun in his negotiations with Commodore Perry, while Perry's coming fired the more the imaginations and desires of those who wished no longer to be shut out from the touch of human fellowship and history, and these inner forces of Japan came to consummation over the question of foreign intercourse which Perry's visit raised in a new and vivid form.

[1] Griffis's *The Mikado's Empire*, pp. 291, 292.

Japan

The Japanese writers mark three distinct stages in their history since Perry's visit. "In the first stage," says one of them, "which may be said to extend from the visit of the American men-of-war at Uraga in 1853 to the Restoration of the Imperial rule in 1868, we were forced by pressure from without to open the country. Mobile and versatile as our countrymen are, it required no little time for them to recover from the inertia of more than 200 years. Those who had the reins of government in their hands soon perceived the utter impossibility of maintaining the policy of seclusion and proposed to acquiesce in the inevitable; but in doing so they had to meet the resistance of irresponsible and ignorant agitators, and the result was the conviction which led to the fall of the Shogunate.

"With the fall of the Shogunate or rather with the establishment of the new Government, the second stage of our foreign intercourse commenced. Active participation now took the place of passive acquiescence. Not only was the country opened, but Western civilization was cordially welcomed and assimilated. Indeed, the overthrow of the Tokugawa regime is a striking illustration of the way in which even seemingly adverse forces coöperated to urge the Nation toward its destination. In the beginning, the Tokugawa Government favored opening the country, while the Imperial Government at Kioto was the centre of the party hostile to foreign intercourse. From this it would appear that the restoration of the Imperial rule was the triumph of the anti-foreign spirit, but such was by no means the case. The Shogunate fell, not because of its liberal foreign policy, but because the division of the country into petty provinces under the feudal system, and the existence of an actual ruler by the side of the legitimate sovereign had become unbearable. So long as the Government was concerned exclusively with internal affairs, the inconsistency of the military rule of the Shoguns with the rightful claims of the Emperor was not manifest, and the people were generally content. But from the instant the country came into contact with the outer world, the unification of the Nation under one intelligible head became an absolute necessity, and the anti-foreign movement was the chief agent in affecting this unification, though the agitators themselves may not have been conscious of it. . . . That movement, after it had once identified itself with the cause of loyalty to the legitimate sovereign, did not stop until the Shogunate was overthrown, without

Japan

reference to the views entertained by its leaders regarding foreign policy. And (thus) when the Imperial authority had been restored, the first act of the new Government was, perhaps unexpectedly but none the less naturally, to announce its intention to adopt a most liberal and progressive foreign policy. The Tokugawa Government was destroyed, but the policy of opening the country survived the catastrophe.

"Since the Restoration, not only has the country been opened to the world, but it has striven to take its due rank among the civilized States. It need scarcely be said," continues the Japanese authority I am quoting, "that it has been with this very purpose in view that the barriers to foreign intercourse have been gradually removed. The consolidation of the Nation was also of paramount importance, and political and social reforms have been chiefly directed toward this end. The abolition of the feudal system and the establishment of an irresistible centralized Government were as a matter of course needed for the unification of the State. Industrial enterprises have been encouraged as a means of strengthening the country. Intellectual activity has been stimulated, that the people might equip themselves with the knowledge essential for competition with foreign nations. Restraints on religious belief have been taken away, in order to give a new departure to the moral life of the people, adapted to the new conditions growing out of foreign intercourse. Finally, the recognition of the rights of the masses and the progress of political liberty point to the appreciation of the fact that the whole people, not a particular class, must be counted on for the promotion of the interests of the Nation."[1]

This second stage melted into the third when in 1889 the Emperor issued the constitution, established a Parliament, and swore that "having by virtue of the glories of his ancestors ascended the throne of a lineal succession unbroken for ages eternal" he would guarantee and defend to his people the rights then acknowledged. In the years that have elapsed since, the cry of the land has been "Greater Japan," "National expansion," "Foreign intercourse on terms of equality," and the incident of the war with China has strengthened in Japan as it has vindicated in the eyes of many nations the claim for foreign recognition on equal terms. In this final result, the consummation of the whole struggle and aspiration since 1868 or 1843, "we may safely say," observes a

[1] *The Far East*, Vol. i., No. 2, pp. 1–4.

Japan

Japanese writer, "that the position obtained by our country is without precedent. So far as nations of non-European origin are concerned . . . it seems to be left for Japan to show that the sphere of civilization may be supra racial. In this we have a mission. . . . We shall strive to widen the range of our common civilization first by assimilating it, and then by transmitting it to the great body of Eastern countries."[1]

But if foreign intercourse has been thus the directing principle of Japanese history and its goal for fifty years, what gave the idea of foreign intercourse such a hold upon the desires and imaginations of the people? Although much the same external influences played upon China, China remained obdurately wedded to the old idea of exclusivism. What led the two peoples to choose divergent ways? Undoubtedly the character and education of the people. China had been trained for more than two millenniums to regard herself as the Middle Kingdom to which as to Joseph's sheaf all the others came and made obeisance. She acknowledged no dependence on others and no indebtedness to them. She had originated, never borrowed, save Buddhism and to that she gave a new character. As the Em-

[1] *The Far East*, Vol. I., No. I, p 8.

peror Yung Ching said once to a deputation of foreigners, "China will want for nothing when you cease to live in it, and your absence will not cause it any loss." Or, as a Canton proclamation of 1884 declared:

> "All dealings with foreigners are detestable,
> These men have no father or mother,
> Their offspring are beasts."

Japan on the other hand had received the whole substance of her learning, institutions and customs from without, and her people had the capacity and the willingness to receive. Long centuries spent in adopting foreign views and ways from the Continent had given them the capacity, and the traditional desire of the people for what is best had fostered the willingness. It is this character springing from education and disposition that has made the Japanese so open to the idea of foreign intercourse. Some call it their fickleness, especially when making this comparison which we have just made with the Chinese; but, as Dr. Verbeck, who knew the people and the language as well as any man, wrote shortly before his death, "This charge of fickleness needs to be qualified. During the feudal regime, for about three centuries, they surely were sufficiently steady and conservative. The Chinese as a nation have not yet emerged from that kind of stag-

Japan

nancy, whereas the Japanese have entered on the path of human progress. The present generation of Japanese lives and moves in an age of change in all departments of life, in an age of transition from the old to the new. In things material as well as immaterial they are making for something better and something higher than what they were and what they had by heredity and transmission from of old. The Japanese are quick-witted and apt to jump to a conclusion without sufficient knowledge or examination; hence they readily enter upon a thing quite new to them. It does not take them long to find out that they have made a mistake, or perhaps they are disappointed while at the same time it is likely that another good thing has attracted their attention. And so they go in for that, and so on. But by and by, when they have finally hit upon the right thing they are quite steady and often splendidly persevering." Or, as they themselves say, "We are bound to have the best and we will try and try until we find it." While the Chinese have said, "We have always had the best, known the best, and been the best. We are the best now. To consider change is disloyalty, unpatriotism and supreme folly." So the roads have diverged.

Missions and Politics

On this open-minded, pliable, receptive people two tremendous forces played. One was the pressure of Western civilization in trade. The merciless relentlessness of this I think we little appreciate in this land, and especially in this atmosphere. The whole enginery and ingenuity of Western Nations, diplomacy, intimidation, flattery, deception, bribery, kindness, enterprise, friendliness,—every known influence has been used to support and enlarge the trade of the West. The heroic figure of the century in the minds of Europeans in China and Japan is Sir Harry Parkes, because of the fearless audacity with which during a long career he took these Nations by the throat and trained them into respect for Western trade and into a willingness to buy the goods of Birmingham, Manchester and India. This intimidation veiled itself or ceased early in Japan, but in peaceable and respectful ways continued to press the Japanese people with almost irresistible power into fuller contact and larger dealings with the trading peoples of the West.

But it may be questioned whether the other force was not even mightier than this;—the sentiment of progress, of desire for recognition, and for the possession of those elements on which equal intercourse was supposed to depend. And

Japan

it may be maintained that it was in Christianity and the influence of Christianity that the sentimental forces as contrasted with the sordid, culminated, and were brought to bear most practically upon the efforts and ideals of the Nation. It was under the impact of Christianity upon the people that the first impulses of the new national life were shaped. Scarcely any one had a greater influence upon these than Yokoi, the chief counsellor of the Lord of Echizen, who was a member of the new cabinet formed by the Emperor in 1868, on the fall of the Shogunate. The five articles which the Mikado then took oath to enforce were proposed by one of Yokoi's disciples. 1. The formation of a Congress or deliberative body. 2. The decision of Government measures according to public opinion. 3. Abolition of uncivilized customs. 4. Impartiality and justice displayed in nature to be made the basis of action. 5. Intellect and learning to be sought for throughout the whole world to establish the Empire. These ideas Yokoi had imbibed from the American constitution and institutions, and from the Bible, a copy of which in Chinese he had got from the missionaries in Shanghai. Before he had seen a missionary in Japan, when there were no Christians of whom he knew and no church,

Missions and Politics

Yokoi wrote to a friend, "In a few years Christianity will come to Japan and capture the hearts of the best young men." Before his assassination in 1869, because of his sympathy with Christianity, he had proposed the elevation to citizenship of the outcast Etas, had pled for freedom of speech and press, and the equalization of taxation, and had sown the seeds of the great ideas which were settled in 1889 in the present constitution of Japan.

If this is assigning too great influence to Yokoi, it is not to Christianity. "New Japan," declares one of the most sober foreigners in the Empire, "is largely a product of Christian influences." While Western science and art, home politics and journalism, foreign travel and commerce, manufactures and industries on foreign lines were in their infancy and had attracted the attention of few people; when there was barely yet an idea of an Imperial Parliament, political parties had not yet been organized, army and navy had no existence, there were no railroads or steamboat companies, few newspapers, and when foreign diplomatic relations came within the scope of but a few officials, and the minds of the people were open and free of all preoccupation, while a great company of Samurai, stranded by the fall of feudal-

Japan

ism were waiting for the touch of a new interest, Christianity swept a hand over the chords of the national heart, sounded a call to the people to enter the great Christian brotherhood, and promised in Christianity the forces that would make the Nation anew and secure its entrance into the councils of the civilized peoples. Doubtless the personal response to Christianity as a message of individual cleansing and redemption was comparatively slight; but the Nation thrilled at it as the summons and invitation of civilization, and under its influence its new life took shape. Japan set about the absorption of the institutions of Christendom, postal, legal, political. Even their old calendar was given up and the Gregorian calendar of Christendom adopted, and the Christian Sunday made a rest day for all officials and for the teachers and officers of the public schools. "The personal influence of Christian statesmen of America, England or Germany," wrote Dr. Gordon,[1] "over Japanese statesmen has been deeply felt and acknowledged. It is, for example, an open secret that when Count Ito, who afterward framed the national constitution, visited Germany, he was remarkably affected by the evidently sincere declarations of the

[1] Gordon's *An American Missionary in Japan*, pp. 228, 231.

Missions and Politics

Emperor William and Prince Bismarck that the Christian religion is essential to the prosperity of Japan. . . . Not only the public men and institutions of Christendom, but the private home life of Christian families also, has profoundly impressed Japanese students and others visiting the Occident. The influence of Christian books has been incalculable, (such as) Wayland's 'Moral Philosophy,' Northend's 'Teacher and Parent,' and Dr. Wines's writings on penology (for example). . . . Christian civilization has achieved and is achieving a great victory physically, intellectually and morally," in Japan. Especially marked was this victory in the establishment of the present educational system. Christian men from America organized it, established the great University at Tokyo, and inspired the first Imperial Educational Rescript in 1872, which declared: "Although learning is essential to success in life for all classes of men, yet for farmers, artisans and merchants and for women it was regarded as beyond their sphere; and even among the upper classes aimless discussions and vain styles of composition only were cultivated. Much poverty and failure in life is owing but to these mistaken views. It is intended that henceforth education shall be so diffused that there may not be a village with an

Japan

ignorant family, nor a family with an ignorant member."

In this way the new Nation and its institutions were established. Viscount Mori Arinori proposed that English should become the language of Japan. And even men who were not missionaries soberly suggested that Japan might become Christian by Imperial Edict any day. Professor Chamberlain did so.[1] And as for the missionaries, only ten years ago they sent out an appeal containing these words: "This then is our opportunity; such an opportunity as the Modern Church has never had vouchsafed to it. A century ago was heard once more a divine voice saying, 'Go teach all nations.' And men asked, 'Whither shall we go?' To-day a man stands upon the shore of Japan crying, Come over into Asia and help us. And we must go now. . . . Other nations may wait. . . . This course will go far toward ending our work in the Empire. . . . By the close of the century . . . Foreign Missions may give way to Home Missions. . . . So far as we are concerned, the Gospel of the Kingdom will have been preached as a witness in Japan. And when

---

[1] Chamberlain's *Things Japanese*. Art. *Missions*, p. 241.

that is done the Church at home will be free to go elsewhere."

Thus in our day, or literally in one generation, a nation was to be born out of Confucian feudalism and Buddhist hopelessness into English civilization and Christian life. Has it been? What is Japan to-day? With what are we reckoning when we deal with the Japanese in the present politics which are rolling out in unchangeable history so fast behind us? Let us try to answer these questions.

A member of one of the legations said to me, "We have always had confidence in the statesmen who really guide Japan, and nothing has occurred to shake our confidence in them. They are level-headed, sober and modest, knowing that they have a great deal to learn, plenty of necessary growth before them, and a big problem on their hands." That these men make their mistakes of judgment, including moral judgment, is natural, but those who have the best opportunity to judge, believe that they want to do what in the courts of civilization would be regarded as honorable and right. Such testimony should be accepted. And in a sense these men are the real Japan. They are the authoritative voice of the country to the Nations without, and they guide

Japan

and restrain as well as they can the Nation within; but in a sense they are not the real Japan. It is not their spirit that is the assertive spirit of the Nation. Neither is it the spirit of the great mass of the people which represents the real Japan. Of this great mass, constituting seven-eighths of the population, perhaps the vast majority are unaffected by the rapid ebb and flow of public opinion, and retain the olden spirit or simply follow their leaders. The class that is constantly expressing itself on the platform and in the press, and in public and private life is between these extremes, and constitutes the Japan that is seen and felt and to be dealt with. It is broken up into parties and schools, but it can be broadly characterized.

First: Industrialism is undoubtedly the chief note of its present spirit. At first Western civilization seemed to consist in the external forms and these were absorbed. Then it was thought to lie in education and religion, and it was held that only as a Christian nation would Japan be admitted to the circle of civilization. Then political institutions must be adapted to those of the West. Armaments and the spirit of war followed, and the secret was supposed to lie in them; but at last the real basis of civilization has been found, and without surrendering any of her other discoveries except her desire for the foreign religion, Japan has launched out into commercialism with an energy and enthusiasm that are marvellous. Since 1886 her exports have trebled and her imports quadrupled. In the same time the value of the machinery imported annually has increased tenfold, and the available horse-power of the machinery in the country from 1,105 in 1884, to 29,493 in 1891, and 61,252 in 1895. In the last ten years prices have risen fifty per cent., and during the last six months, since the adoption of the gold standard, have risen higher still. "The predominant trait of the day is industrialism," said a leading Japanese to us, "the aristocracy of money. The trader used to be despised. He was below the artisan and the farmer. Now in the estimation of the people the great merchant is above officials. . . . The people are mad for money to spend on food, drink and pleasure. We are becoming a grasping Nation." "No," said others, "the Nation sees that wealth is the secret of national power. We would be a great Nation. To be a great Nation we must be rich." This materialistic spirit fills the land now. As evidence, while we were in Japan, there appeared an article on *America's Opportunity in Japan* in a

Japan

Japanese magazine, containing these statements: "There is nothing that country (of America) is unable to buy or undertake from lack of funds. Their eyes are widely open to money making; to them money making is the standard of everything. Carlyle's sarcasm on the English people 'whose hell is the want of money or the failure to make money' is very true of the American people, and there is a certain charm in that. They are eager to make money and to enrich the country, hence there are magnificent educational and charitable institutions and industrial progress. Doubtless it is this money-making spirit that made America what it is now. . . . The Japanese spirit of looking ahead and grasping the newest things in the world cannot be satisfied elsewhere so well as in America. To-day, whichever way we may turn we can see the influence of American progress stamped in the Japanese material civilization. Then remembering this fact, if Americans will concentrate their time, interest and money that they have to spare to Japan, in the commercial, industrial and agricultural lines, they will give a lasting and permanent influence to Japan, and one that will be more beneficial to them than the missionaries' attempt to save souls (here) and to give them the promise of bliss in heaven hereafter."[1] It will be evident that the missionaries are not the only American influence at work in Japan. It is interesting to note also that the writer of these baldly materialistic lines, Watari Kitashima, was nourished in the bosom of the American Church, having been graduated from Allegheny College and the Meadville Theological Seminary of the Methodist Church. The dollar is to be the new deity of Japan. The long talk about an eclectic and adapted religion, the freshest child of progress, has at last come to fruition in a coin.

Second: "National pride, a false sense of honor as individuals and as a Nation is the second characteristic of the present spirit of Japan," said one of the Japanese I have already quoted. "The war with China led to a great development of this, but its real source was in Confucianism fostered but modified by our feudal system." Some expressions of this exaltation of sense of mission and of national self-esteem must be given. It was especially evident, of course, in connection with the war. One Japanese wrote in *The Japan Mail*, "Some 15,000,000 of helpless souls kept ignorant and defenceless to satisfy the jealousy of the world's most backward nation! Could this

[1] *The Far East*, Vol. ii., No. 6, pp. 255-258.

Japan

be borne by lovers of freedom and reverers of human rights? Japan's victory shall mean free government, free education and free commerce for 600,000,000 souls that live on this side of the globe. The war we have entered on is a righteous war." I suppose that in literal fact, no war was ever prepared for so perfectly, so uninterruptedly, with such cool selfishness. Now that the war is over, and its civilizing schemes have collapsed so ignominiously, the Japanese are still full of plans for the civilization of Asia, and a foremost place among the nations. A leading article in the *Kokumin-no-Tomo's* English edition says, "When we find something more advanced or better than what we have, we do not hesitate to throw away and grasp at the other. The miraculous progress of modern Japan is attributable to this disposition. She has not only appropriated the Occidental civilization, but also modified or rather improved it in some respects by means of Oriental ideas. In commerce, in industry, in art, in science, nay in every respect, we have been showing that we as a Nation are not a bit less gifted than our Western friends. . . . Their admiration is now changing into awe. See how closely the so-called civilized nations are following our post-bellum measures, such as the protection of the mercantile marine, the encouragement of manufacturing industries, and the enlarged schemes of our army and navy! Some of them are guarding against our armament, and others are warning against our commerce and industry, and others are hopelessly casting an evil eye upon us. An anti-Japanese sentiment is peeping out in everything and everywhere. No doubt the world is not destined to be the exclusive theatre of the white actors. The Creator, if there be a Creator, did not create the other races to be permanently employed as mere waiters or slaves of the white races. It is the grandest mission of the children of the Rising Sun to preach that the world was made for all and not for a limited number of races or nations. . . . Thus we see that it is not the 'Asiatic' but the Japanese ascendency that the Americans fear. . . . The chief motive that led the Americans to undertake the annexation (of the Sandwich Islands) is the anxiety about the Asiatic ascendency." Count Okuma, the new Prime Minister, in a public speech some time ago, went even further than this, declaring " The European Powers are already showing symptoms of decay and the next century will see their constitutions shattered and their empires in ruins. Even if this

Japan

should not quite happen, their resources will have become exhausted in unsuccessful attempts at colonization. Therefore, who is fit to be their proper successors if not ourselves? . . . If treaty revision were completed, and Japan completely victorious over China, we should become one of the chief Powers of the world, and no Power could engage in any movement without first consulting us. Japan could then enter into competition with Europe as the representative of the Oriental races."[1] Another writer goes even further, and suggests that Japan is to be the Savior of the United States. "What patriotic American," he asks, "fails to see that the Nation which introduced Japan to the world needs recreation as well? . . . An influence akin to that reflected across the Atlantic, may reach America across the Pacific, and much of demagogism, mammonism and rummism, together with dissensions in religion may lose their power by such an influence." Here and there a protest is raised against this flood of inflation, but in many cases these protests are born of self-satisfaction and self-assurance, and it is not unjust to characterize the present spirit of the Nation as one of unmitigated conceit. "The great need of Young Ja-

[1] Norman's *Peoples and Politics of the Far East*, p. 392.

Missions and Politics

pan," said one foreign resident, "is the application at each meal of an efficient spanking machine."

Third: Commercial and conceited, Japan is made with militarism. It surpasses even Russia and Germany. The spirit of arms is nourished from one end of Japan to the other. It fills the schools, which are drilled and marched from the lowest grades. The youngsters have wooden guns. The larger boys are regularly armed. They may be seen almost daily on their parade grounds at drill, chanting the national anthem as they march, countermarch and charge. "Her educational system," says Lafcadio Hearn,[1] "is an enormous drilling machine." The school girls cry aloud to the war spirit, one of their papers bursting forth, "Yamato warriors! We praise you! You who never flinched in times of greatest danger, nor fled from the enemy, but gladly sacrificed your lives for the cause of the Emperor and your own country. What hardships you endured as you made your toilsome way, barefooted, through snow and ice, while bitter cold winds penetrated your clothing. Japan must become great; she must become the light of the Eastern world; her future is the future of all Ori-

[1] Hearn's *Kokoro*, p. 96.

ental Nations, and upon her civilization their civilization depends. The peace of our Nation is the peace of the Eastern world, and any nation interfering with that peace is an enemy that must be crushed. . . . For that reason alone have our brave warriors shed their blood upon the battlefield."[1] The army now numbers nearly 300,000, and the plan is to double it by 1902, and to have the navy doubled by 1906. Already there are as many officers in the Japanese standing army as we have hitherto had private soldiers in ours.

Fourth: The spirit of nationalism has grown more intense as the years have passed, and breaks out now and then in sharp anti-foreign feeling which the long delay of Western Nations in surrendering their rights of extra-territoriality has embittered. Anti-foreign feeling rests either on the sense of supreme superiority as in China, or on the sense of inferiority, or on the idea that a nation is regarded as inferior by others. Both of these latter grounds exist in Japan, as the *Jiji Shimpo*, Mr. Fukuzawa's paper, frankly acknowledges: "Japan must make up her mind to let go the old and open her hands unreservedly to the new . . . abolishing everything that tends to preserve racial prejudices, and thereby to handicap her in the

[1] *Kwassui Quarterly*, Aug. 1, 1896.

struggle toward progress." Many have a lurking sense of the inferiority the *Jiji* avows. Irritation is unavoidable.

In the present temper of the Japanese mind the spirit of national assertiveness is of necessity the spirit of foreign antagonism, for it is not an assertiveness as toward an ideal she is striving to realize, but a struggle for the recognition she wishes to receive from Western Nations. Her ideals are second hand. For a while this foreign antagonism was simply psychological or an idea in politics. Since the China War it has been translated into ships and guns and army corps. These have no internal meaning. The young men say they are meant for Russia[1] and the great struggle that must come, but the spirit of the young men is hot and precipitous in Japan. At any rate, nationalism, or anti-foreign feeling —its synonym—is now embodied in iron and flesh, and waits.

Toward civilization stripped of all personal and national relations, no force in Japan save the old religions opposes itself now; but toward the national and personal forms in which civilization is and has to be met there cannot but be an unrestful feeling. For Japan herself is not civilized yet,

[1] Hearn's *Kokoro*, p. 108.

Japan

if we accept at all as we must, such a definition of civilization as Chief Justice Russell gave at the American Bar Association's meeting in 1896, "By its fruits you shall know it. It is not dominion, wealth, material luxury; nay, not even a great literature and education wide-spread, good as these things be. Civilization is not a veneer; it must penetrate to the very heart and core of societies of men. Its true signs are thought for the poor and suffering, chivalrous regard and respect for woman, the frank recognition of human brotherhood, irrespective of race or color, or nation or religion, the narrowing of the domain of mere force as a governing factor in the world, the love of ordered freedom, abhorrence of what is mean and cruel and vile, ceaseless devotion to the claims of justice." Few of these signs are evident in Japan yet. Indeed such a definition condemns many of our Western Nations. While Japan has become a nation of strength and of position, the change though a real and a permanent change, is not a moral and vital change in such a sense as to entitle the Nation to be called civilized. And all comparison with other peoples shows her this, or shows her that other peoples think this, which amounts to the same thing for the purpose.

Missions and Politics

And now fifthly, the two things most needed by Japan in this emergency are most conspicuously lacking. One is a solid morality. *The Japan Mail* charges that the native papers do not hesitate to misrepresent facts. A foreigner of some years residence, writing in a Japanese magazine says: "As viewed by foreigners Japan has no commercial morality, no business character." The last census reports for 1895 365,633 marriages and 110,838 divorces. Many declare that they do not know one Japanese whom they would trust to teach ethics in a school, because of distorted, ingrained ideas of honor, truth and falsehood, relations and position of woman, etc. Japanese scholars even contend that Oriental morality "avoids the vagueness that characterizes Christian teaching" and is distinctly superior to Christian morality. The other great need is, a pure and reasonable religion. How soon Japan forgot her initial leaning to Christianity, how superior the new Japan has been to any sense of this need, and how great the need is, are all illustrated by the now familiar words of Marquis Ito in an interview in the *London Daily News:* "I think most of the educated Japanese prefer to live by reason, science and the evidence of their senses. I have secured absolute toleration for all religions, and to a certain extent I would encourage a spirit of religion, but I regard religion itself as quite unnecessary for a nation's life. Science is far above superstition, and what is any religion, Buddhism or Christianity, but superstition, and therefore a possible source of weakness to a nation?" As over against this madness two Japanese papers may be quoted: *The Kokumin Shimbun*, "Great crimes are becoming more frequent. Cases come under our notice daily. The country feels keenly the necessity of morality and religion. Those who have hitherto attached themselves only to a materialistic form of civilization and believed gold to possess almighty power, have now begun to rely on religion for the preservation of social morality. . . . It is almost safe to conclude that the whole Nation feels the necessity of religion. We ourselves have no connection with religious parties (How characteristically Japanese!) but we do firmly believe that religion is absolutely necessary to society, and that along with materialistic progress spiritual progress must go hand in hand. We are not at all sorry, therefore, that the country has begun to feel the necessity of religion." And *The Yorozu Choho*, "Japan's case is that of Christian civilization without Christian-

Missions and Politics

ity. She is aiming at a definite form of organization without the life that organized it. The peculiar awkwardness of her present position is due to her hopeless attempt to assimilate the new civilization to her old ideals." Another paper speaks of "the spiritual disease of our people." Unfortunately all of these, while containing an element of prophecy are, in the main, academic meditations. The editor who deems religion necessary for the Nation does not intend to make any personal application. The Japan which I am describing is most adroit at diagnosing itself; but it is without a religion and without any fixed body of principles, eager after science, facts and ideas, but wanting any moral foundations, fast losing even its old virtue of reverence. "Buddhism has reached the height of corruption and has no influence among the upper classes. Shintoism retains only a feeble influence. Christianity which was once rather powerful, has lately become more or less lifeless," adds one of the papers I have quoted.

Yet, though I have made this quotation in support of what has been said about religion in Japan, I do not believe that any one of its three statements is true. Buddhism is denounced as doomed. So it is, but distantly. In the five

Japan

years preceding the last census, the Buddhist preachers and priests increased from 93,253 to 101,839, while the Shinto preachers increased from 69,300 to 98,451. In no other land we visited did Buddhism seem to have the hold it had in Japan. Nowhere else were there such temples, so steadily thronged, so gloriously decorated, so filled with priests, so supported by ecclesiastical colleges, with the idols so venerated, the offerings of money so profuse. Nowhere else did we meet priests so well informed, so adroit in apologetic, so well armed in advance against the points of special strength in Christianity. The sister of the Empress is the wife of a Shin Shiu Buddhist priest, and all through society the relations of the people to Buddhism are close. The social life of the Nation is intershot with it, and it is working with great ingenuity, with imitation of Christian methods, and with almost as great readiness to compromise and adapt as it showed when it came to Japan thirteen hundreds years ago. And the chief incentives in this Buddhist revival are found in the nationalistic feelings already described. "The religions which are back of the evils imbedded in the social life of the country are made to appear synonomous with the most sacred and time-honored institutions of the land,

Missions and Politics

the very basis of loyalty to the throne itself."[1] This ground is taken especially in the interests of Shintoism, the distinctly national cult, which looks back hazily to the dimly seen gods of old, and reduces itself practically to an ambiguous worship of the imperial idea personified in the Emperor.

"Is it possible," asks a writer in one Japanese magazine, "to reconcile the idea of the sacredness of the Japanese Emperor with the doctrine of Christianity which teaches that Christ is the supreme Governor of all things, both visible and invisible?

"Is it not against the very Constitution of Japan to recognize supreme beings such as a God, a Jesus, a Pope, a Church or a Bible, other than the sovereign of the country?

"Do Christians mean to regard Jesus as a faithful subject of the Japanese Emperor, or do they mean to bring down the latter under the rule of the former so that he might offer the prayer saying, 'Jesus, the Son of God, have mercy upon me'?"[2]

As a matter of fact, popular opinion is without

---

[1] *Seventeenth Report of the Council of Missions Coöperating with the Church of Christ in Japan*, p. 10.

[2] Quoted by the Rev. J. H. De Forest, D. D., in *The Independent*, Feb. 10, 1898, pp. 5, 6.

Japan

anchorage, without fixed principles. The real old religions have lost their hold on the educated, but they have been metamorphosed so as to justify their use by the educated as vantage ground from which to work for nationalism and this use has reacted to revive the old religions in their old form among the common people. In the absence of any solid principles those who have really lost faith are clutching at all things. Eclecticism gone mad runs through their books and papers. All the lessons of history are thrown away, and having absolutely no guiding moral principles, men gather all sorts of truths, half truths and falsehoods together and out of them try to make something that they can call Japanese, and that will serve as that religion whose absolute necessity they will be forced to see, yes, are even now discovering for themselves. The abyss of a French Revolution will never open in Japan.

Why was it that Christianity which started with such bright prospects has not already become the religion of the whole Nation? Twenty years ago the churches were thronged, the missionaries were overrun and some of them almost adored; the schools were crowded and thousands were pressing into the Church. For a while the Church doubled each three years. But it was not

Missions and Politics

all a solid movement. The real causes were not all spiritual. The availability of Christianity as a liberal influence, its connection with Western civilization, the attractiveness of its ethics, the novelty of its doctrines and its methods, the necessity of its acceptance to full Western intercourse, the example of the enthusiasm of the Christians and of the changed lives of real converts, the fascination of the new learning opened up in the Mission schools, the high character and remarkable intelligence of the missionaries, and the fact that Christianity had at first a clear field were the chief reasons for the tremendous leap into popularity Christianity made. For ten years or more it steadily gained ground and then the reaction came. The causes of the reaction were partly negative and consisted in the subsidence of the influences that had lifted Christianity into power and prominence. The pace of the people had quickened into a passion. Western civilization was discovered, as it was believed, to be independent of Christianity. The ethics of Christ naturally lost their attractiveness in a land where one of every four marriages issues in a divorce, and among a people into whose very fibre and tissue un-Christian ideas and standards have been knit and twisted and woven for centuries. The

Japan

novelty wore off its doctrines, and Buddhism plagiarized its methods. The supposed necessity of its acceptance to full Western intercourse aroused resentment against it. The enthusiasm of the Christians began to wane as the tide ebbed, and the unchanged lives of supposed converts began to counterbalance the changed lives of real. Government schools better equipped and minus Christianity, showed that the sweets of the new learning could be had unalloyed by religion. The secular claims of civilization crowded in upon Christianity, and the missionaries were at last believed when they said they were but men and brothers. So the mists were dispelled and the dream was done.

But the reasons for the reaction were not wholly negative. A feeling grew up that it was not seemly to show such undignified haste in accepting Western things, and it was easy to single out Christianity as the one thing which should be debarred. It could better be given up than the wonderful material gifts of the West. And then the rationalism of the West poured in like a flood. What wonder that it shook Japan out of her drift toward Christianity and made the Church quiver to her foundations. Less than a generation out of the old life of Japan, with no inherited equipment

Missions and Politics

of moral and intellectual tendency drawing them to the truth, struggling themselves for a solid foundation of faith, beaten as by the billows of a great storm by surge after surge of error and fancy pouring on them from Christian lands, a little handful, misunderstood and maligned, perplexed by the conflict of influences they could not stop to scrutinize and slay at cool leisure, dazzled and bewildered by the lights that flooded them, swung along constantly by the mad rush of the Nation, the Christians of Japan have been fighting their battle against not heathenism only, but heresies born in Germany and Great Britain and America, against materialism learned by the Japanese in our own marts, against evolutionary notions of religion and ethics and the philosophic struggle against supernaturalism which have come to them as the most advanced thought of the most advanced nations. This has been their Church history. Where has there been one like it? I do not wonder that the catastrophic hopes of the earlier days have died slowly away, and that men have to recognize now at last that in Japan as elsewhere, the coming of the Kingdom of God is without observation, and that its day has not dawned.

But it will dawn. It is true that "the Japanese

Japan

are frivolous, are lacking seriousness, are little affected by the grave or the sublime; are too fickle to know true placidity of mind, and too callous to escape from falling into cold indifference," that they have never heard a Moses or one of the prophets, nor seen the righteous God passing by, that "they have delighted to paint Fugi-yama, their sacred mount surrounded by birds and flowers, and have regarded the happy man as the highest man, that they have need to learn of Moses and the prophets that fire is the fitting garment of the holy mountain, and that the highest man is the Man of Sorrows." It is true that "they have no fifty-first Psalm in their language and no Puritan in their history," and that, "they need to be awed, to be smitten into seriousness, by the revelation of the God who is above the world and of the hell which is underneath civilization, and of the Christ whose eyes are as a fire."[1] All this is true, but it is true also that God holds them in the discipline of His holy will, and that with all sincerity they want what is best. Who dare doubt that they will find it at last with all their national hopes and boastings—nailed to a cross?

There is something which kindles enthusiasm

[1] *Contemporary Review*, April, 1892, Art. "*Christianity in the East.*"

Missions and Politics

in the vision of this eager, straining people. It is sad to see them grasping at the fruits of civilization and ignoring its unseen but indispensable roots. But it quickens faith and adds a keen interest to the long-sealed life of Asia to mark this young Nation, protesting that it is younger than the Anglo-Saxon, stepping out so boldly into the untried ways. It was almost ready to lead Asia, propounding a Monroe Doctrine for the continent of our distant fathers, as we have propounded one for our own. Even yet perhaps to the drum beat of Asiatic federation it will guide the ancient peoples out into the land of promise. Perhaps in the cold, hard bitterness of war, the great Colossus of the North will crush and stifle all its buoyant hopes. Perhaps the future will be like the past, check and counter check, in the petty game of national banter and pride, while underneath the Kingdom of God builds and builds, while He that keepeth Israel slumbers not nor sleeps. We can wait and see. Meanwhile let us not be of those who speak contemptuously of God's dealings with a people to whom as well as to any people, the words which John Milton spoke 250 years ago of England apply: "Consider what a Nation it is! A Nation not slow and dull, but of quick, ingenious and piercing spirit;

Japan

acute to invent, subtile and sinewy to discourse, not beneath the reach of any point the highest that human capacity can soar to.

"The shop of war hath not there more anvils and hammers working, to fashion out the plates and instruments of armed Justice in behalf of beleaguered Truth, than there be pens and heads there, sitting by their studious lamps, musing, searching, revealing new notions and ideas wherewith to present, as with their homage and their fealty, the approaching reformation; others as fast reading, trying all things, assenting to the force of reason and convincement.

"What could a man require more from a Nation so pliant and so prone to seek after knowledge? What wants there to such a towardly and pregnant soil but wise and faithful laborers to make a knowing people, a Nation of prophets, of sages and of worthies? We reckon more than five months yet to harvest. There need not be five weeks. Had we but eyes to lift up, the fields are white already."

LECTURE V

Korea

> "We sleep and wake and sleep, but all things move,
> The Sun flies forward to his brother Sun;
> The dark Earth follows wheel'd in her ellipse:
> And human things returning on themselves
> Move onward, leading up the golden year.
>
> "Ah, tho' the times when some new thought can bud
> Are but as poets' seasons when they flower,
> Yet seas, that daily gain upon the shore,
> Have ebb and flow conditioning their march,
> And slow and sure comes up the golden year.
>
> "When wealth no more shall rest in mounded heaps,
> But smit with freer light shall slowly melt
> In many streams to fatten lower lands,
> And light shall spread, and man be liker man
> Thro' all the season of the golden year.
>
> . . . .
>
> "Fly, happy happy sails . . .
> Fly happy with the mission of the Cross;
> Knit land to land, and blowing heavenward
> With silks, and fruits, and spices, clear of toll,
> Enrich the markets of the golden year.
>
> "But we grow old. Ah! when shall all men's good
> Be each man's rule, and universal Peace
> Lie like a shaft of light across the land,
> And like a lane of beams athwart the sea,
> Thro' all the circle of the golden year?"
>
> TENNYSON, *The Golden Year.*

LECTURE V

KOREA

THE future political historian, looking back upon our century will range its incidents and movements with reference to its two great impulses,—the development of Democracy and the dominance of European States in Asia. The inner history of every civilized nation will find its explanation for him in the former, and in the latter he will discover the key that will open many of the secrets and intricacies of diplomatic intercourse and national jealousies or collusions. Other matters have of course entered, like the partition of Africa, but that question has been of the same nature and has indeed been only incidental to the problem of Asia whose trade routes were involved in the control of Egypt and the Cape. And even the Napoleonic movement which may seem at first sight not sufficiently explicable by the movement of Democracy and the development of the Asiatic problem, had its vivid relations to each. One of the most interesting chapters in the history of the century has to do

Missions and Politics

with Napoleon's supposed attempt to lay the foundations of Empire in Asia, and Sir John Malcolm's efforts to frustrate such designs at the court of Fath Ali Shah at Teheran.

The network of problems connected with the designs of Europe upon Asia men have called for two generations "The Eastern Question." Stripped of all cant and complication it is simply the question of the supremacy of European Nations in Asia, and the limitations and adjustments of their supremacy. The time has not come yet for writing its history. Indeed its history has only begun, and no man can unravel now the great tissue of deceptions, encroachments, honest purposes, irresistible drivings of destiny, briberies, duplicities, adaptations of Eastern methods by Western energy, jealousies and just dealings which have surrounded it thus far. Some future generation will be able to read the fascinating story, and to wonder at the blindness of this century to the distinctions between facts and fictions, and at its readiness to fight for imaginations and vague suspicions while it smilingly endured real ills and grievous wrongs.

The generation that is thus able to read with luminous clearness the history of our century, while wondering at our narrowness of view and

Korea

our curious distortions of judgment in many matters, will, on the whole, perhaps, admire the democratic movements in which the people have come to their inheritance as kings and priests unto God. On the other hand, it is to be feared that it will view with sadness, as we regard the wrongs of the Middle Ages which yet led up to the dawn of modern liberty, the selfishness and injustice of most of the aggressive forces in the Eastern Question; though it will recognize, as we can do now, that they led on toward the coming of the Kingdom of Righteousness.

It is because I believe that these forces are doing this, through no purpose of theirs but under the overruling will of God, that I have spoken so much in this course of lectures of them, and of the way the Mission force is working under and through them, as in India, or so largely in spite of and against them as in China and Japan; and for this same reason and because it is well for us to study the workings of God in our own time, I come now in this last lecture to speak of one of the latest developments of the Eastern Question, and its close relation to the missionary development of the Church in Korea.

It is most interesting to note the way in which the Eastern Question in Asia has moved steadily

Missions and Politics

Eastward. Early in the century, the seat of controversy and diplomatic competition was in Persia. France was supposed to be working toward India and intending to make Persia and the Persian Gulf her highway thither. England's efforts to prevent this supposed movement through a treaty with Persia which declared outrageous treatment of the French to be Persia's duty and which resulted in a firman, directing Persian Governors to "expel and extirpate the French," and "to disgrace and slay" them as intruders have been denounced by Sir Henry Rawlinson, later British Minister to Persia, as "an eternal disgrace," and he speaks with equal contempt of England's subsequent course in violating her treaty obligations to Persia and abandoning the poor wreck when she discovered that nothing was to be feared from Persia and nothing to be gained. The seat of conflict and controversy in the Eastern Question had shifted.[1]

Men supposed next that it was to be settled in the Turkish Empire, and the Sultan has been bolstered up to this day on that supposition. Therefore the Crimea, the Balkans, Egypt, Bulgaria, and the curse of the Ottoman still in Europe. It was on this supposition that the

[1] Rawlinson's *England and Russia in the East*, Chaps. i., ii.

Korea

Eastern Question was to be solved in Constantinople that Stratford de Redcliffe, with all the good he did, did also this wrong of laying on firmer foundations under the rotten throne of the Sultan the jealousies and rivalry of England and Russia, and that Disraeli and Salisbury at Berlin so tied up the Ottoman Empire to British responsibility that by that token it stood and defied all Christendom, while it slew 100,000 Christians, including their little ones who had done no wrong. Yet neither has the Eastern Question been solved at Constantinople nor has all the struggle of Great Britain prevented the slow but certain passage of the Sultan and his city under the power of the Slav.

Then again it was supposed that the Eastern Question, which since the fall of Napoleon has been mainly the dual struggle of England and Russia, would be fought out among the Afghans. England pushed her Indian frontiers to the Indus, and refusing to accept Lord Lawrence's plan[1] to make the banks of the Indus her boundaries, pressed on to Peshawur and the passes to Afghanistan; while Russia creeping steadily from the Caspian Sea, past Khorassan, through Bokhara, overhung ominously from the North. Kan-

[1] Boulger's *Central Asian Questions*, p. 129.

Missions and Politics

dahar, Kabul, Herat and Merv became the steels from which the flints of conflicting interests struck showers of sparks; but the Eastern Question has not been solved or concentrated in the Afghan mountains, though the two Powers draw closer and closer there, Russia's last outpost being practically at Faizabad, and England's at Chitral and less than 150 miles separating these two.

But meanwhile the Eastern Question had moved further East and by way of the Pamirs, Sikhim, Kuldja, and Peking focused itself afresh under our eyes in Korea. No nation seemed less likely than Korea to be lifted thus into prominence—the Hermit Nation, opened to Western intercourse for only fifteen years, a relic of Chinese customs, dress and opinions left over from the times of the Mings before the Tartar conquest, curious, antipodal, remote from Constantinople, Teheran, Herat and Peshawur, the vast majority of its people ignorant of all of these names, scarcely a hundred of them acquainted with the existence of the Eastern Question, a small peninsula bordering only barren territory, wanting nothing from any one and of little value to any one—how did this little kingdom come to be entangled in the meshes of this old problem? Strange as it may seem at first sight, a little glance over history is

Korea

sufficient to remind us that Korea has been for centuries the pivot of political movement in the Far East, and that it was inevitable that the Eastward movement of Europe which constitutes the Eastern Question, should clash sometime with that "course of empire" which was Westward bound long before Bishop Berkeley by a quatrain fixed the eyes of the world upon its march. Where else should this contact occur than in the little kingdom which has ever been the centre of the great movements of Eastern, Central and Northern Asia?

The history of Korea runs back to the time of King David. On the broad, richly fertile plain to the West of the present city of Pyeng Yang, the walls and the wide, straight streets of the city of Keja or Ki tse are still pointed out, hidden in part when we were there, by the luxuriant crops of millet and other grains. Keja was David's contemporary.[1] The Shang dynasty in China had ended in Chow Sin, the "Nero of China" who died in 1122 B. C. Keja was one of his nobles, and remonstrating with his master for his tyranny was cast into prison. Released by Chow Sin's successor, Keja refused the office of Prime Minister lest he should be regarded as

---

[1] *The Korean Repository*, Vol. ii., No. 3, pp. 81-87.

Missions and Politics

condoning the revolution which had overthrown the tyrant, and removed to Northern Korea. His story may be legendary, but the Koreans believe it, and told the American Admiral, John Rodgers, in 1871, that "Korea was satisfied with her civilization of 4,000 years and wanted no other." After ten centuries of independence Keja's line became vassals of China under the Han dynasty in the second century B. C. By the second century of our own era, an independent kingdom had grown up again through the conquest of Keja's old territories by a race from the North, and this new Korean kingdom not only maintained its independence but overthrew with complete disaster the Chinese armies which from time to time invaded the land, prior to the seventh century of our era. While the kingdoms of Northern Korea were thus struggling with China, the Southern kingdoms of the peninsula were dealing with Japan, and were sending over to her their religion, philosophy, political institutions, products and arts. Early in the third century, the Queen of Japan invaded these kingdoms, subdued them, and is said to have written on the King's gate, "The King of Shinra is the dog of Japan." Thereafter the Southern Koreans paid tribute to Japan until the whole peninsula was

Korea

unified under one of the Northern Kings named Wang, in the tenth century, and formed an alliance with the Sung dynasty in China to which the Koreans agreed to send tribute. When Genghis Khan arose, the Koreans became his vassals, and two Mongol invasions thoroughly subjugated their land, which Khublai Khan also made the base of his vain attempts to conquer Japan. When the Mongol Empire broke up and the Ming dynasty succeeded it in China in the middle of the fourteenth century, Korea came under its vassalage and the present dynasty was established on the throne. This ended the old relations between Southern Korea and Japan, and thenceforth Korea became the middle ground between Japan and China, their common place of meeting and conflict, while Korea's alliance with the Mongols had further embittered the Japanese against her.

In the five centuries which have elapsed since the Korean Government was remodeled after the fashion of the Mings and passed under their suzerainty, there have been repeated attempts of Japan to subjugate the peninsula, and she has probably never in all these years abandoned the design of detaching the kingdom from China and attaching it to herself. The late war as we shall

Missions and Politics

see, was no accident or avoidable struggle, but a step, abortive as it now seems, yet a step prepared for and contemplated for years, for generations, for centuries, and never lost sight of in all the changes through which Japan has passed, toward a continental enlargement of her Empire.

The first of these invasions was at the close of the sixteenth century when the Shogun Hideyoshi sent an army of 150,000 Japanese, the best soldiers of that age in Asia, to overrun Korea. The Chinese sent armies to resist. After weary years of fighting, the Japanese poured in a second invasion, but though Korea was desolated it was not subjugated, and in 1598 the Japanese armies were recalled, retaining only Fusan, on the Southern coast, which was theirs until 1876, and which they practically hold to this day.[1]

From the Chinese side also poor Korea has been harassed. Less than twenty years after the withdrawal of the Japanese the Manchus assailed the Ming dynasty, and the struggle began which put the present rulers of China on their throne. The Koreans did not know which way to turn, and they trimmed and compromised and faced two ways until the Tartars came down on them like a flood, forced their allegiance, and displacing the

[1] Griffis's *The Hermit Nation*, Part i.

Korea

Mings imposed on the Koreans a heavier vassalage. This, combined with the tribute they had been paying also to Japan, would have been too heavy a burden if the Japanese also had demanded increase, so the Shogun excused them from a heavier levy, and gradually the hold of China strengthened and the influence of Japan weakened, until in 1832 the tribute to Japan ceased.

The Manchu dynasty forced some changes upon China, but remembering the assistance finally rendered them against the Mings by the Koreans, left them undisturbed and the old ideas and ignorance of the times of the Mings continued to hold full sway in Korea. The influences which opened China scarcely affected the Koreans. They did not feel at all the passions which shook Japan. Until our own day Korea remained closed and unknown save from curious and unreliable stories of shipwrecked sailors and reports of the Roman Catholic priests.

The doors were opened only fifteen years ago, and the steps which led thereto were in part analogous to the pretext upon which Germany has appropriated Kiao Chou Bay in China. Korea would have been opened in any event, but its opening was hastened by the last great massacre

Missions and Politics

of Christians in 1866. The Very Reverend Father Wallays of the Societé des Missions Etrangères, of Penang, who has written an interesting account of their missions in Asia,[1] says that as early as 1592, during Hideyoshi's invasion, Japanese Christians "were able to announce the true religion to their Korean prisoners," but the zeal of Father Gregory de Cespedes among the people in 1594, met with no success. For two centuries practically nothing was accomplished although the Catholic priests at Peking are said to have taught from time to time the ambassadors whom the King of Korea sent to bear the annual tribute. Toward the close of the last century, however, a group of students, seeking enlightenment, interested themselves in Christian books which had found their way in from China. This led to visits to the Catholic missionaries in Peking, fresh supplies of books with crucifixes and images and in the conversion of a number of men who in the absence of any priest baptized one another, took Christian names, and organized a Church patterned so far as they knew after the Roman order. The movement spread, and in spite of persecution and the banishment and beheading of the leaders, numbered, it is said, 4,000

[1] *Missions Etrangères*, trans. by E. H. Parker, pp. 94-136.

Korea

Christians in 1794, the year in which the first foreign priest, Jacques Tsin, a Chinese, reached Seoul. The inhibition of ancestral worship in 1791, led first to opposition and on the death of the king, Chang Cheng, in 1800 and the accession of the queen, a general royal edict against Christianity was issued "which was to be writ with letters of blood in the annals of Korea," says Father Wallays' chronicle. In spite of a second edict and continued persecutions there were said to be 9,000 Christians in 1838. In 1839, another edict was issued and the three European priests in the country were executed. In 1857, the Catholics numbered 16,500. Political elements had crept in already, however, and these were more pronounced when the news of the defeat of China by France and England in 1860 arrived. It was feared then that the armies would come to Korea, and "in many instances people of rank humbly sought the good favor and protection of the Christians. Medals, crosses and books on religion were bought in quantities. Some even wore them publicly on their dress, hoping for safety when the dreaded invasion should come." More priests came. Christians multiplied until 1866. That year was the year of martyrdom. A letter came from Peking from the Korean am-

Missions and Politics

bassador there, declaring that the Chinese were killing all the Christians in the Empire. In Seoul an anti-foreign spirit was dominant. It was determined to follow the great example of China. Of four bishops and nineteen priests, fourteen fell as martyrs, and thousands of native Christians were slain. Many eyewitnesses in Korea tell the story of those bloody days when the sands of the Han River were red with the blood of those who were faithful unto death. The Tai Wan Kun, the father of the present King, and until his recent death the most disturbing element in Korean politics, conducted these last and most furious persecutions, and never relented until the hands of civilization pushed open the closed doors which concealed his iniquities. To revenge the great massacre a French naval expedition came toward the close of 1866, but it failed wretchedly, left the impression that it had been overwhelmed and only instigated the Tai Wan Kun to a more determined effort to exterminate Christianity root and branch. "It is for the sake of the Christians," said the official proclamation, "that the barbarians have just come here. It is on account of these only that the waters of our river have been defiled by Western ships. It behooves that their blood should wash out the

Korea

stain." The same impression was produced in China, and some trace the Tientsin massacre three years later to this unfortunate expedition.[1]

It was this same year that our relations with Korea began, although we had indirect relations long ago when Jonathan Edwards at Stockbridge was annoyed by the drunkenness of his Indians, who obtained their money and drink from the Dutch traders at Albany, in exchange for ginseng root which the Dutch took down to New York and shipped to Korea.[2] Our direct relations were inaugurated by the destruction of an American schooner, the General Sherman, which ran aground in the Tatong River near our Mission station at Pyeng Yang, and was burned by Koreans who also murdered her crew. Our Government sent a man of war to obtain satisfaction, but failed, and dispatched four years later, a small expedition which captured the Korean ports at the mouth of the Han, killed some Koreans, but did not get to Seoul, and withdrew, leaving with the Koreans a stronger conviction than ever that the Western Nations were, though troublesome, afraid and harmless.

By this time Japan had passed through her new

---

[1] Griffis's *The Hermit Nation*, Part iii.
[2] Griffis's *The Hermit Nation*, pp. 388, 389.

birth, and as soon as the new Government was organized and a department of Foreign Affairs created, the Korean Government was summoned to resume ancient friendship and vassalage. "This summons," as Griffis says, "coming from a source unrecognized for eight centuries, and to a regent swollen with pride at his victory over the French and his success in extirpating the Christian religion and irritated at Japan for cutting free from Chinese influence and tradition, was spurned with defiance." An insolent reply was sent to Japan, but the Nation was not yet ready and the insult was pocketed, though the coming punishment of Korea was thenceforth more distinctly than ever the first goal of Japanese foreign policy, and in 1876 an unwarranted attack on some Japanese soldiers led to the invasion of the peninsula. There was no war, however. China, which in peaceful times claimed Korea as her complete vassal, and in difficulties disavowed all responsibilities for her, gave the Japanese Minister in Peking a written disclaimer of responsibility for the outpost state, and even sent a messenger to Seoul advising the young King who had taken the government from the Regent, to accept the first of the alternatives Japan offered—a treaty of commerce or war. Korea

Korea

chose as China advised, and Article I. of the new treaty read, " Chosen being an independent State enjoys the same sovereign rights as Japan." Three ports were opened as a result of this treaty, and for a time progressive influences seemed to prevail in Seoul. At any rate both by China and by Japan Korea had now been declared free and independent. But China had not the least idea of so regarding her, and within Korea the conservative elements were far too strong to allow an easy breach with Chinese vassalage and antiquity.

Still, while the progressive party was in power the spirit of foreign intercourse was given some play, and the Japanese treaties were followed in 1882 by treaties with America and China, and these were followed by British, German and French; and then came an outburst that threatened to destroy all that had been secured. The Tai Wan Kun was at the bottom of it, having fostered the anti-foreign, anti-progressive spirit in every way, teaching the people that "the Japanese were inebriated with the manners of Christian Nations and were enchanted by the Western devils, and that as a Europeanized country was being created in their immediate neighborhood, they must expel the barbarians." The people arose, many of the family of the Queen

Missions and Politics

Min, a strong, progressive woman, were killed, and the Japanese were driven out of Seoul.

The doors had been opened, however, never to be closed again, and in a few months the Japanese were back, an indemnity of $500,000 had been agreed to by Korea and subsequently remitted by Japan, and the Tai Wan Kun kidnapped by the Chinese envoy was carried off to China, where he would find things antiquated to his taste, while a number of Chinese soldiers remained in the country to preserve order. So Japan and China drew near and faced one another in the affairs of Korea once again,—the progressive party counting upon Japan's sympathy, and the reactionaries upon the aid and coöperation of China.

The first clash came in 1884.[1] The liberal party planned a scheme including the murder of the leading conservatives and the initiation in Korea of a progressive movement like that in Japan. It was thus that the affair began, but it ended in a pro-Chinese, anti-progressive demonstration which brought back the Tai Wan Kun, threw the Government into the hands of the conservatives, and by convention between China and Japan re-

[1] *The Korean Repository*, Vol. iv., Nos. 3, 4, 6, Articles by F. H. Mörsel on The Émeute of 1884.

Korea

moved their armies on equal terms, with this provision which led to the late war, that " either China or Japan should have the right to dispatch troops to Korea, if necessary to preserve order or protect their subjects, on giving notice each to the other, and that when order was established both forces should be withdrawn simultaneously."

The seeds of the late war were in that convention, as a few years showed, for the country went slowly on from bad to worse under the rule of the Confucian party in the State. There is absolutely no hope for a nation wedded indissolubly to worn-out forms and arid ideas, and at last an uprising came in the form of a revival of the Tong Haks, or " Eastern Students " a name they took in 1859 when the sect arose under a man named Choi who had meditated on the spread of the Roman Catholic Church, and had professed to have received a supernatural revelation that it was not the true religion, but that there was one God who was to be worshipped. His religion was a mixture of Confucianism, from which he took the Five Relations; Buddhism, from which he took the law for heart-cleansing; Taoism, from which he took the law of cleansing the body from moral as well as from natural filth;

and Christianity, from which he borrowed the term and idea of God. The name "Eastern Learning" also he chose in contradistinction to So Hak or Western Learning or Romanism. Choi was beheaded under the charge of being a Romanist in the massacre of 1865-1866, and the Tong Haks were put under the ban; but they have never been suppressed as a sect of virile, monotheistic protestants against corruption or tyranny, a sort of Korean Tai Pings.[1]

In the Spring of 1893 a party of them came to Seoul from the South with accounts of oppression and wrongdoing, and a petition that the dead Choi should be declared innocent and have a certain rank and a name and a monument. The King refused their petition, and in 1894 the uprising came. The Tong Haks swept across Southern Korea as the Tai Pings had swept across Central China, only with perhaps a more sincere purpose to rid the land of its incubus of sterile Confucian leeches, and set it free for some sort of clean government.

This was the appeal they issued to the country: "The five relations of man in this world are sacred. When king and courtier are har-

[1] *The Korean Repository*, Vol. ii., No. 2, pp. 56-60; Vol. ii., No. 6, pp. 201-208.

monious, father and son loving, blessings follow and the Kingdom will be established forever. Our Sovereign is a dutiful son, a wise, just and benevolent ruler, but this cannot be said of his courtiers. In ancient times, faithfulness and bravery were distinguishing virtues, but the courtiers of to-day are degenerated. They close the ears and eyes of the King so that he neither hears the appeals of his people, nor sees their true condition. When an attempt is made to get the truth to the King, the act is branded as traitorous, and the man as a malefactor. Incompetency marks the men in Seoul, and ability to extort money those in the country. Great discontent prevails among the people, property is insecure, and life itself is becoming a burden and undesirable. The bonds that ought to exist between king and people, father and son, master and slave, are being loosened.

"The ancients say, 'Where ceremony, modesty, virtue and righteousness are wanting, the Kingdom cannot stand.' Our country and condition is now worse than it has ever been before. Ministers of State, governors and magistrates are indifferent to our welfare; their only concern is to fill their coffers at our expense. Civil service examinations, once the glory of our people, have become a place of barter; the debt of the country remains unpaid; these men are conceited, pleasure-loving, adulterers, without fear; and the people of the eight provinces are sacrificed to their lust and greed. The officials in Seoul have their residences and rice fields in the country to which they propose to flee in time of war, and thus desert their King. Can we endure these things much longer? Are the people to be ground down and destroyed? Is there no help for us? We are despised, we are oppressed, we are forsaken, but we still remain loyal subjects of our gracious King. We are fed by him, clothed by him, and we cannot sit down idly and see the country disgraced and ruined. We, the people of the whole realm, have determined to resist unto death the corruption and oppression of the officials and to support with zeal and courage the State. Let not the cry of 'traitor' and 'war' disturb you. Attend to your business and be ready to respond to this when the time comes."[1]

By patriotic appeals and other methods not so scrupulous the Tong Haks raised rebellion, not against the King, for neither progressive nor conservative has ever renounced him, but against the corrupt official class, and by June, the capital of

---

[1] *The Korean Repository*, Vol. ii., No. 1, pp. 29-35.

Korea

Chulla Province had fallen into their hands. Upon this the King appealed to China for assistance in putting down the rebellion. If the progressive party had been uppermost in his councils at the time, the appeal would have been to Japan. China at once responded, and announced to Japan the departure of the troops in accordance with the convention of 1885, asserting also in her note that Korea was her tributary State. Japan at once sent troops also, and challenged the claim to suzerainty over Korea. It is unnecessary to trace the steps that followed in detail to fix the precise responsibility for the war. Mr. Norman charges it upon China. Others charge it upon Japan. The simple fact is that, it was certain that Japan had never abandoned the idea of controlling Korea either as a vassal state or as a state independent of China and under the tutelage of Japan. If one justification for a war to this end had been wanting, another would have been found; and plenty being at hand and hostilities having already begun in which Japan had occupied Seoul at the cost of some Korean lives and sunk a Chinese transport bearing more troops to Korea, formal declaration was made by the Mikado on August 3, 1894.[1]

[1] Norman's *Peoples and Politics of the Far East*, Chap. xxiii.

Missions and Politics

Under Japanese influences Korea had already given notice of the renunciation of all conventions with China and all claims of China upon her, and had promised reforms in the Government. In two months the war was over, and Korea had slipped out forever from her old moorings and was moving out into the future in the wake and under tow of Japan. Japan had embarked on her mission of civilizing Asia, and had now one nation absolutely in her control for good or for ill.

She kept Korea for just one year, and it cannot be denied that she set a pace of progress and reform that took the breath out of her ward. Japan had crowded the whole history of civilization into one generation in her own case. She seemed bent on lowering this record with Korea. In the main her influence was most exemplary. She purged the offices of the State. It was estimated that over 17,000 persons were struck off the pay rolls in three months—chiefly attendants, eunuchs, gatekeepers, retainers, etc. The Government was reorganized into departments, with genuine duties and responsibilities, and records were opened, past administrations having left no records, having done nothing worth recording. Courts were established in which justice was ap-

Korea

plied. Taxes were regulated and no longer left to caprice. Salaries were fixed to all official positions, and bribery, office buying and all squeezing were abolished. Trade was encouraged. Accounts of Government revenue were established, and an annual budget of expense and receipts inaugurated. All that Japan had learned from civilization she was eager to teach Korea; but the temptations of the situation were too great, and the impatience of the teacher could not be restrained. She forgot that great changes need time and that civilization is a growth from within and not a garment thrown on from without; and forgetting this and intoxicated with the joy of reform, she began to vaccinate the people, and to cut their hair, to prescribe the width of their sleeves, and the cut of their trousers, and yet while pleased as a child with the chance of teaching the mint and anise and cummin of progress, by no means lost sight of the weightier matters of the law.[1] Naturally a people schooled for centuries in Confucian notions, comatose with Chinese conservatism, even though startled by the overthrow of their old patron and the meteoric demonstration of the superiority of Western

---

[1] *The Korean Repository*, Vol. iii., No. 7, pp. 263-272; Vol. iv., No. 5, pp. 192-195; Wilkinson's *The Korean Government*, passim; Bishop's *Korea and Her Neighbors*, Chaps. xxxi., xxxii.

ways, did not like to be hustled along in this fashion. The Japanese on the other hand, became convinced that they could get Korea civilized yet more rapidly if the Queen, who was not a reactionary woman, but only a careful, shrewd, patriotic stateswoman, could be disposed of. The idea was simply monstrous, but it was actually carried out, and the Japanese Minister deliberately arranged for the murder of the Queen. It was an outburst like the savagery at Port Arthur during the war, and shows how much is yet to be done in the transformation of Japanese life and character.

The deed was done early in the morning of October 8, 1895. On the preceding evening Japanese influence was absolutely supreme in Korea, but no one loved it. The reforms had provoked even the people most benefited by them. Japan had executed them in the most obtuse and unconciliatory way. No party had been built up favorable to Japanese influence. The dismissed officials loathed their rulers, and the common people were incensed at their dictatorialness. The murder of the Queen was the match. The explosion followed. One wonders at the stupidity of the Japanese in committing such a blunder. Any one could see the temper

Korea

of the people. Every one knew also that the Queen, even though she might be slow and cautious, was the most reliable and intelligent element in the State, and the best guarantee of such progress as was made.[1]

But the blunder was committed, and in twenty-four hours Japan's influence in Korea was dead. The King fled to the Russian legation, and the country passed without an effort on his part or the expenditure of one rouble or one life into the hands of the Czar. And so the Eastern Question, the most disturbing and harassing question of the century, rose up grimly in the Land of Morning Calm. And yet for a time, the wise, tolerant, honest course of a Russian Minister in Seoul gave good promise that the question would not be freighted there with jealousies and conflicts and threats of strife. He gave the King a temporary home, aided him in his course, discouraged him from injustice, advised the employment of an Englishman as financial adviser of the Treasury, with more power than he possessed for himself, dealt with firmness, moderation and self-restraint toward all, and then unfortunately was transferred to Mexico, and a new man of a different

---

[1] *The Korean Repository*, Vol. ii., No. 10, pp. 386-392; Vol. iii., No. 3, pp. 118-142; Bishop's *Korea and Her Neighbors*, Chap. xxiii.

Missions and Politics

type came on the scene, and for a season seemed about to abandon his predecessor's policy, and to turn the Eastern Question in Korea into the same question that has frowned for two generations on Afghanistan.

In 1887, to secure the evacuation of Port Hamilton on the Korean coast by Great Britain, the Tsung li yamen gave England assurance that the Russian Government had given a "most explicit guarantee, distinctly declaring that in the future, Russia would not take Korean territory." But Great Britain, herself, gave solemn assurances that she would retire from Egypt. As surely as Egypt is not to be surrendered by Great Britain, or almost as surely, control over Korea's destiny will not be surrendered by Russia. The prize is in Russia's keeping and at Russia's disposing. That is the sovereign political force that will control Korea's destiny, whatever temporary conciliations may be given to Great Britain or Japan.[1][2]

---

[1] Curzon's *Problems of the Far East*, Chap. vii.

[2] The latest development of the relations of Russia and Japan to Korea is indicated by the Protocol agreed upon, April 25th, 1898, as follows:

Article 1. The Imperial Governments of Japan and Russia definitely recognize the sovereignty and entire independence of Korea, and mutually agree to refrain from all direct interference in the internal affairs of that country.

Article 2. Desiring to avoid every possible cause of misunderstanding in the future, the Imperial Governments of Japan and Russia mutually agree, in case Korea should apply to Japan or to Russia for advice and assistance, not

Korea

But there is another force at work in the making of Korea, and its operation is most marked. It entered at the time of the upheaval of 1884

to take any measure in the nomination of military instructors and financial advisers without having previously come to a mutual agreement on the subject.

Article 3. In view of the large development of Japanese commercial and industrial enterprises in Korea, as well as the considerable number of Japanese resident in that country, the Imperial Government will not impede the development of commercial and industrial relations between Japan and Korea.

The following opinions from two Japanese papers will serve better than anything else as commentaries on this agreement. They are reported in the *Japan Weekly Mail* for May 21, 1898.

"The *Yorozu Choho*, calls the recently concluded Russo-Japanese Protocol mere 'nonsense.' In the first place, Russia will not pay any attention to its provisions when it suits her convenience to disregard them. She snapped her fingers at the Yamagata-Lobanow Convention the moment that she saw her account in so doing. In the second place, it is not Russia but Japan that the Protocol hampers. Russia finds it irksome at present to meddle with Korean affairs. The Manchurian problem occupies her entire attention. Had she been persuaded to sign this Protocol at the time when it suited her policy to fix her grasp upon Korea—last spring, for example—the document might have been regarded with some satisfaction. But now that she has voluntarily stepped out and left the field clear for Japan, the result of such a Protocol is to prevent the latter from utilizing the situation as she might have otherwise done. Russia having already determined to stand aloof in the interests of her own convenience, concedes nothing when she embodies her abstention in a document. But Japan concedes a great deal when she agrees that her hands shall be fettered which would otherwise have been free. That, stated briefly, is the gist of the *Yorozu Choho's* comments on the first two articles of the Protocol. With respect to the third, it inquires what possible right Russia would have had under any circumstances to oppose the development of Japanese trade and industry in the peninsula. She could have had no such right, and it is consequently absurd to pledge her not to exercise it. On the whole, our contemporary concludes that the profits conferred by the Protocol belong solely to Russia. Japan has been thoroughly befooled."

"The *Jiji Shimpo* has a remarkable article on the subject of the relations between Japan and Korea. It will be remembered that the *Jiji* strongly advocates the settlement of Japanese in Korea, being persuaded that no better plan offers for the development of the latter country and the spread of Japanese influence there. Our contemporary now urges the importance of

Missions and Politics

which drove the liberal leaders out of the country. The missionaries were obliged to exercise the greatest caution at first. Dr. H. N. Allen, who is United States Minister now, was only able to

inducing Buddhist priests also to cross to the peninsula and take part in the movement of colonization. This advice is not tendered on religious grounds so much as on account of the humanizing and tranquillizing effect of missionary teaching and example. Very great differences exist between the customs, traditions, language and methods of the Koreans and the Japanese. It is inevitable that these differences should become causes of friction, and that all kinds of misunderstandings should arise. The influence of Buddhist missionaries would be invaluable under such circumstances. There is considerable similarity between the conditions that may be anticipated in Korea and the conditions that existed in Japan thirty-five years ago. Japanese visiting Korea will be chiefly bent upon the pursuit of gain and will not be disposed to pay much attention to the sentiments and customs of the Koreans, or to allow their spirit to be controlled by any consideration for the country or the people. That was the case with foreigners in the early days of Japan's intercourse with them, and there can be no doubt that many serious troubles would have occurred had not the Christian missionary acted as a counterbalancing influence. The Christian missionary not only showed to the Japanese the altruistic side of the Occidental character, but also by his teaching and his preaching imparted a new and attractive aspect to intercourse which would otherwise have seemed masterful and repellent. The Japanese cannot thank the Christian missionary too much for the admirable leaven that he introduced into their relations with foreigners, nor can they do better than follow the example that he has set, in their own intercourse with the Koreans."

The *Japan Mail* comments editorially, "As to the worth of such a declaration, it is useless to say anything. The validity of every pledge depends, to a large extent, upon the good faith of those concerned in observing it. . . . That the promise contained in this new Protocol has been made in good faith, no one has any right to doubt. That it can be faithfully observed in the face of the conditions created by other covenants, appears to us altogether problematical. . . . It is curious to note how completely Japan has stepped into the place hitherto occupied by China *vis-à-vis* Korea. This Rosen-Nishi Protocol bears a remarkably close resemblance to the Ito-Li convention of 1885. It was predicted by good judges at the latter date that if unhappily China and Japan should ever quarrel over Korea, the on-looker Russia, would principally profit by the fracas. The forecast was sound. It is with Russia that Japan has now to parley about Korean independence, as she parleyed with China thirteen years ago. Let us hope that the analogy will never be pushed to completion."

Korea

gain a foothold by acting as physician to the American legation until his fortunate treatment of Min Yong Ik brought him into the favor of the King, and soon thereafter it was possible to do work untrammelled. Especially since the war the Koreans have shown themselves singularly open and adapted to the Gospel. Instead of crying "foreign devil," as foreigners are saluted in China, the Koreans address the missionaries by a title of honor and kindness. Christians are received with remarkable confidence and regard. In the North of Korea the Church has spread and penetrated as we saw nothing to surpass anywhere in the world. We visited one day a large and well furnished temple to the Chinese god of war in Pyeng Yang. The gates were closed and locked, and the pavements were overgrown with grass. At last a keeper, who said he was there only because it was a cheap place to lodge, let us in and showed us the forsaken shrines and the unworshipped gods. "Why is this?" we asked. "Where are the worshippers?" "Oh," said the man, "so many people believe in this Jesus doctrine that no one comes here any more." The country has been favorably impressed by Christianity, from the King who counts some of the missionaries as his most trusted friends, down to the coolies. The Government itself subscribed for 467 copies of *The Christian News*, a weekly paper edited by Dr. Underwood, and ordered them to be sent one to each of the 367 magistracies, and ten to each of the ten departments of the central Government, the King himself receiving his copies. How strong the influence of Christianity has been may be indicated by a proclamation issued by the Governor of Whang Hai Do, one of the best provinces: "Our school was handed down to us by the sages of old days whose teachings and doctrines are forever unchangeable. But of late the foreign religion came into the country; the foolish novelty seekers have fallen into the foreign teaching and they are unwilling to study and observe our own religion. Is it not a danger to our doctrine? I have heard a European say that if one country adopts the religion of another the country will surely be destroyed. I believe it to be true. Even foreigners entertain such a belief and gave us the hint, and we, the disciples of the saintly sages, must not be enticed into foreign teachings which destroy our venerable customs and institutions. I desire our Confucian followers to be more diligent in studying the Classics, making them their true religion, and to regard the new teachings as superficial doctrines. Thus they will all become useful vessels of the State and accumulate great fortunes for the people."

¶ One of the most interesting and striking features of the Korean Church is its patriotism. Our belated coasting vessel deposited us in North Korea on a Sunday morning, and along the Tatong River our attention was called to villages in which on bamboo poles, small Korean flags were flying. Those flags marked the residences of Christians or were flying over churches. It is a practice which has grown up among the Christians without missionary pressure, to run up the national colors over their homes and churches on Sunday. They do it to proclaim the character of the day and to mark their own respect for it. Some of the leading Koreans in Seoul have organized an Independence Club, and have laid out an Independence Park and built an Independence Arch and established an Independence Day,—the 16th day of the seventh Korean month, in celebration of their independence of China brought about through the war. These are the advanced and liberal men. The reactionary Confucianists hunger for the good old iniquitous days, and Russia and Japan look on with interest. The leading spirit in the Independence movement is a

Missions and Politics

Christian. Most of the patriotic demonstrations made while we were in Korea were by Christians. In Pyeng Yang they had a great picnic on Independence Day. No one else observed the day. On the King's birthday, which fell on Sunday, the Christians listened to patriotic sermons in churches decorated profusely with national flags. The next day they had in Seoul a large open-air mass meeting, addressed by Dr. Jaisohn, the leading spirit of the Independence movement, editor of the vernacular newspaper, and a Christian; by the Mayor of Seoul, formerly Minister in Washington, whose wife is a Christian; and by the assistant Minister of Education, a devout Christian, who with Dr. Jaisohn was educated in the United States, and who was a member of the Korean Embassy to the Czar's coronation. On the last Sunday we were in Korea, another great mass meeting was held in a royal building, at which half a dozen spoke, and some of the speeches ran in the same fervent political strain. One spoke on the text which describes the apostolic missionaries as men who were turning the world upside down, and pointed out how in Korea men had been really standing on their heads in the mud. "The missionaries have come to right things. Society must be turned upside down. There is no hope in the upper classes. Christianity begins at the bottom. After all, a man's a man, be he king, noble or coolie." Then a voice in the crowd said, "What kind of talk is this?" "Christianity is no Tong Hak or rebellious doctrine," the speaker went on, "it teaches only to worship God, fear no man and do right." "Whom have we to fear?" asked the next speaker. "Who is there to trust except God? Great men? If you should stick a knife into them it would hurt just as it would hurt me. No, trust God only, and we shall win. Christ's Kingdom will prevail. Where is Alexander's Empire? Where are Greece and Rome? Gone utterly. And where is Christ? Ruling everywhere. It cannot end otherwise. Right and God and Christ will win." "There is no reason," he added, "why we should not expect to see a Christian King on the throne of Korea." Little of such free and stirring speech as this has been heard in Korea before.

The reasons for this fervid patriotism among the Christians are manifold. One is that Christianity has quickened and vivified the minds of the people and given them boldness of speech, so that they see now the abuses of the past and the glory of progress, and are able to reason daunt-

Missions and Politics

lessly about such things. Another is that Christianity is essentially an emancipating religion, and leads inevitably to the desire for free government and peace and popular institutions. Yet another is that the Catholics have always erred in the matter of patriotism, and indeed of being guilty of downright treason to Korea. Coming out into Protestant enlightenment just at the time when Korea was being roughly hustled by Japan into the paths of civilization pretty much against her will; and then seeing Japan's grasp failing and the country standing without true heart or sound mind, the Christians have been roused to speak out boldly for their King, but also for righteous government and just laws. A further reason is to be found in the influence of some leading men who recognize that the only hope of the country lies in the power of Christianity and Christian education. One of these said to us, " The only hope of the country is in the churches. There is no moral character in Korea. It is being created in the churches. There is no cohesion or unity or confidence among men. There is no company of men, however small, capable of acting together. The churches are raising up bands of men who know how to combine for a common object, who are quickened intellectually, and

Korea

are full of character, courage and hope. To convert and educate the common people is the only hope of the land."

With these two forces then, the Russian Government and the Christian Church would seem to lie the future of Korea. Will the forces conflict? Not at present. Perhaps ultimately they will. The Russian consuls used to tell the missionaries in Asia Minor that when Russia came their work would have to stop. And there is no room for evangelical missionaries in the Caucasus. No Russian Minister in Korea has yet taken such a position, but one of the English papers in Japan recently reported from a correspondent that Mr. Speyer entertained "a far-reaching scheme appertaining to the diplomatic policy of the Land of the Morning Calm. The very changeable attitude of the Korean toward foreigners," says the correspondent, the Minister, "views as being mischievous and capricious and can only be reformed by the power of the Church. He has, therefore, decided to introduce the Orthodox Greek Church and encourage Russian priests to go to Korea." It was an ominous prospect, but Christian Missions are sure to have free course at least for some time. Moreover while some would reckon Russia among the retrogressive in-

Missions and Politics

fluences at work in Asia, she stands for order, protection, law; and her industrial ambition is constructing limits for her political absolutism, while emancipation in some form, which must come, may make Russia's influence not so unfavorable to the higher interests of the Asiatic peoples as has been usually supposed. One must not forget either that Russia has not come yet to herself, that the Slav is only approaching his mission,[1] and that the internal throes which are before them will make of the Russian State and of the Greek Church, forces wholly different from those with which we now deal under those names. And when that day comes, though it may be through a baptism of blood and of fire perhaps, there will come out of Russia elements of new and holy power for the reconstructive processes which are building on toward the Kingdom of God.

I have sketched thus in outline the present situation in Asia, the present spirit of the peoples and the present making of its history, endeavoring to assign its true place therein to the force of Christian Missions viewed in their actual present influence and not in their prophetic promise.

[1] *The Contemporary Review*, Jan. 1898, pp. 1-13, Art. "*The Coming of the Slav.*"

Korea

From one point of view such a study as this is profitless if not dangerous—from the point of view of the method of Missions. We are accustomed in our day to seek for the broad ultimate effects of forces, and discovering them often go back to direct our forces more exclusively toward such effects. Jesus' truth, however, is a broad truth, "Whosoever would seek to save his life shall lose it," and it applies not more to individual life than to some impersonal forces. Their greatest results are the results for which they do not directly seek, which indeed they ignore, which they would miss if they did seek them. It is so with Christian Missions. They have not aimed at sociological or political results, but they have produced them. They are the mightiest force in the world in these directions. But they have been this because they have never sought and therefore have found. The instant Missions ceased to view themselves as distinctly a work of individual regeneration and fixed their aim instead upon social or national reformation, their power would be gone, and they would affect neither nations nor society nor individuals, as they do now. And so I say that if we allowed such a broad study as this of the place of Missions in the present making of Asia to deflect our

Missions and Politics

thought from the true view of Missions as primarily a work of individual redemption, and the true method of Missions as primarily a personal persuasion, we should lose more than we would gain.

There are those who would dispute this position. They regard Missions as mass movements, dealing with men in broad, social streams. This is the Roman Catholic view, as it was the Mohammedan. The great object is to commit men by great groups, and so to bring them into conditions where educational influences can be better brought to bear upon them than when detached one by one from the old affiliations. Laying larger emphasis on environment and the education of associations, those who hold this view strive to secure broad movements. They believe that the faith of children or grandchildren little depends on the character of the conversion and motives of their parents or grandparents. As Father Phelan of the Catholic Church says, "While a study of dogma may bring a few highly cultured minds to accept this or that form of belief, the masses must be drawn by the cords of Adam."[1]

The temptations are strong in our day to draw

[1] *The Independent*, Jan. 6, 1898.

Korea

Protestants to this same view. Some Missions have succumbed. A great deal can be said in their defence. But in the end it will mean inevitable loss. The Good Shepherd knoweth His sheep one by one, by name, and the Kingdom of God is to rest on individuals redeemed and not on the quicksands of multitudes superficially changed.

> "Not sweeping up together,
>   In whirlwind or in cloud,
> In the hush of the Summer weather,
>   Or when storms are thundering loud,
> But one by one we go;
> In the sweetness none may know.
>
> "Not pressing through the Portals
>   Of the Celestial Town,
> An army of fresh Immortals,
>   By the Lord of Battles won;
> But one by one we come,
> To the gate of the Heavenly Home.
>
> "That all the Powers of Heaven
>   May shout aloud to God,
> As each new robe of Life is given,
>   Bought by the Master's blood;
> And the heavenly raptures dawn
> On the Pilgrims, one by one.
>
> "That to each the voice of the Father
>   May thrill in welcome sweet,
> And round each the Angels gather
>   With songs, on the shining street,
> As one by one we go
> To the glory none may know."

But if our study is valueless as to Mission method save in this negative way, it is not so as to Mission motive. Not that there is not motive

Missions and Politics

enough in the need of men and the command of Christ. To whomsoever these do not appeal no new motive can speak; but it must be admitted than neither in the need of men nor in the command of Christ has the Church yet found that spring and spontaneity of motive essential to the buoyant and immediate completion of her world-wide work. This is her own defect. Perhaps the motives of the need of men and the command of Christ have been too powerful for her appreciation, and under the awful burden of them she has sunk apathetic and discouraged. In any event there is buoyancy of motive here in the promise written all over the face of history and the page of prophecy and thrust in our eyes by the politics of our own day, that the kingdoms of the world are to become the kingdoms of our Lord and of His Christ and that He is to reign over them forever.

There is motive in the glorious contrast of that prospect with what exists to-day, in the false, jarring conflict of States which call themselves Christian, among themselves and against the weak and defenceless. It is not necessary to go further for illustration than to Lord Brassey's article on "The Position of the British Navy," in the January *Review of Reviews*, (1898) in which

Korea

he says: "To use the words of Lord Dufferin in bidding farewell to the British embassy in Paris, it has become a national conviction, deeply rooted, that in spite of Christianity and civilization no nation's independence or possessions are safe for a moment unless she can guard them with her own right hand." Looking upon our so-called Christian States thus described, how devoutly one prays for the coming of the Prince of Peace, the mighty Counsellor of righteousness, on whose shoulders the Government is to be! Whatever movement promises that coming has new motive power for all who listen with shame to such confessions—or read with shame such a cynical but true statement of current national morality as the following editorial from the New York *Evening Sun* of April 6, 1898:

"THE FUTILITY OF PROTEST."

"It is represented that a part of the Japanese press is disposed to criticise the Government for permitting the annexation of Wei-Hai-Wei by England without protest. But to what purpose would the Government protest? The Japanese press is said to be so simple as to base its demand for protest on the ground that Japan was turned out of China on the pretext that the integrity of that Empire must be preserved; now the Powers that turned her out are dividing among themselves the identical territory. It is not easy to have patience with flimsy puerilities of this sort, especially when brought forward as a basis for action. Japan should get its 'Æsop' by heart, and inwardly digest that immortal wisdom. When the wolf gave reasons for dismembering the lamb, his doing so was an act of redundant courtesy, for, as a commentator has pointed out, no obligation lay upon him to justify his partiality for chops. So, when the Western Powers alleged the integrity of China as a reason for expelling Japan, they did so out of an excess of diplomatic courtesy. The pretext imposed on no one at the time. The whole world knew that the Powers meant themselves to appropriate the territory, and the reason they proffered Japan was a concession to the graces of intercourse, even if it did demand faith in the phenomenon of water running up hill. The precept, Let your yea be yea and your nay nay, was in the first place directed against profane swearing; in the next, it was addressed to persons in a crude and rude state of society; in the third, it is subversive of the first and greatest of principles, namely, that business is business.

Korea

"In the intercourse between the Western and the Asiatic Nations there is and there can be but a single fundamental basis, that is, battleships. A protest based on battleships is business; a protest not backed by battleships is the sort of thing you look for from attorneys-at-law, school professors and other common scolds. As a proceeding, it is deficient in dignity. Japan is not yet rich enough to have enough battleships; she must have patience. The next seventeen years will do much for her. Combining an artistic taste that France envies and copies with the sturdy tenacious industry of England and a frugality that is Asiatic and all her own, Japan is accumulating capital hand over hand.

"To that purpose she must adhere steadfastly for the present—putting money in her purse. Not until after she shall have money enough can she have battleships enough. In that day her 'protest' will come to stand for something. Meantime, there is nothing for it but to work and save and build up the business. Get battleships by ones, by twos, by threes—they will make a fleet in the end. Grudges laid up now will lose nothing by keeping. Is there not a fable showing a lion and bear lying exhausted, torn and bleeding on the ground while the sly little fox drags off the carcase of the kid whose possession they disputed? Let Japan have patience—patience and shuffle the cards, and put money in her purse with steady inflexibility."

When we turn to this contact of Western States with Asiatic Nations, we feel, surely, more and more deeply the value and absolute necessity of the movement which is preaching among these Nations the Kingdom of Righteousness, and become sensible of the motive power its purposes contain. Captain Mahan speaks in a recent magazine article, with great conviction of this. He calls attention in that article to "the general outward impulse among all the greater nations except our own, shown in their colonizations, shown in their efforts to gain territorial dominion in other lands; and he speaks of the coming together of the Orient and the Occident on the basis of common ideas of material advantage, without the sympathy, the corresponding sympathy, in spiritual ideas. And here he finds a danger, a danger menacing our civilization; for as he says emphatically the civilization of modern Europe has grown up under the shadow of the Cross, and everything that is best in it still breathes the spirit of the Crucified; and there is peril in bringing together the East and the

Korea

West on the basis of common material advantages (or political relationship) without this correspondence in spiritual ideas. Then he adds, justly and profoundly, that if this correspondence in spiritual ideas is to be attained it must not be by a process of growth, but by a process of conversion."[1] Whatever movement—and there is but one—promises to secure this clutches us and our Western Nations with the powerful motive of self-preservation.

"I was exceedingly interested," said Bishop Creighton of the Church of England, recently, "a little time ago in going to a meeting—I think of the Calcutta Mission—which was addressed by Mr. Bryce, who was asked to address it because he had just been to India, and had seen something of the working of the Mission there. Well, Mr. Bryce spoke with great weight, of course. He said that his journey in India had at least convinced him of this, that unless England could succeed in Christianizing its Indian subjects, that Empire could not last; that nothing else whatever could hold it together; that at present there were two sets of lives, two civilizations, two races simply in juxtaposition; that there could

[1] Address of Richard S. Storrs, D. D., before The American Board, Oct. 14, 1897, p. 4.

Missions and Politics

be no real interfusion of the two, and no real possibility of either one understanding the other, except on the religious side; that unless you try to understand men as religious beings, you do not get on from any other side at all. For there is the root of their life, the root of everybody's life—it must, after all, be his religious ideas. However debased his religion may be, you can only understand a man through his religious life, and benefit him by giving him a right religious idea. There is no other way of benefiting mankind at all. All else is simply from the outside, and has no basis of purpose."[1]

But more positively, the course of thought we have pursued together fosters new motive because it shows to us the rising walls and battlements of the Kingdom of God which it is His purpose to establish on the earth. The precise method of its final coming need not concern us. It is enough that Jesus and His conquest are to come, that the King and the Kingdom of God are to be with men and that we can give ourselves to their coming. "Of that kingdom we are the heralds and the pioneers; to secure its universal and enduring supremacy on the earth is our high task; not to set up an 'imperium in

[1] Quoted in *The Missionary Review of the World*, March, 1898, p. 227.

Korea

imperio' but to lodge in human nature and in social institutions (and in the core of life) throughout all the continents and isles of the sea such a knowledge and love of righteousness (and of the Righteous One) as to make the world the abode of purity and peace."

As Dr. Behrends once said, "Our philosophy of human life has been altogether too meagre. Our estimate of history has been singularly inadequate. (For) we have been disposed to regard the present life as full only of vanity, as indeed it is to him who uses it mainly for eating, drinking, getting rich and being merry. But *now* is the accepted time, *now* is the day of salvation. The future has no dignity that does not fill each passing hour, and eternity is the pulse, the throbbing pulse of time. The last days are upon us, in which God has spoken to us by His Son. And, therefore, the present life is not a temporary scaffolding, but the deep and broad foundations God is laying by human hands for the temple of His building; and the history slowly syllabling itself . . . is the first and formative chapter in the glorious records of eternity. The present, prosaic earth is the territory we are summoned to subdue to the obedience of Jesus Christ; the tenants . . . (of eternity) need not be the objects of our solicitude, as they certainly cannot be the objects of our ministry. Here where sin threw down the gauge of battle and made man an exile from Paradise, the conflict is to be fought out to its bitter end, until Eden comes back with a fairer and a perennial beauty," . . . the cry of the poor answered; the meek inheriting the earth; every crushing burden loosed; every yoke of oppression broken; ignorance supplanted by the wisdom whose beginning is the fear of the Lord; lust cast into the bottomless pit; the idolatries and cruelties of paganism swept away, and its weak and sinful people made subject to the holy God, whose voice is in the thunder which rends the mountains, in the gentle breath of conscience and in the law which giveth wisdom to the simple. Under the leadership of Christ, "and with His Gospel in our hands, we are charged to found the Kingdom of Heaven, everywhere and among all men, to supplant sin by holiness, ignorance by knowledge, hatred by love."[1]

Could men find anywhere a grander, holier aim than this, an aim more glorious, more full of thrilling and divine appeal? And there is no more solid and emphatic lesson from the pres-

[1] *The Independent*, June 10th and 17th, 1886.

Korea

ent situation in Asia than that this should be our aim and that God means it to be realized. There is enough that is antagonistic and discouraging, the dawn of the day of God may still be far away, but while we build in the heavy darkness of gloom and the storms of strife, whoso will may

> "Hear at times a sentinel
>   Who moves about from place to place,
>   And whispers to the worlds of space
> In the deep night, that all is well:
>
> "And all is well, though faith and form
>   Be sundered in the night of fear:
>   *Well* roars the storm, to those that hear
> A deeper Voice across the storm."

www.ingramcontent.com/pod-product-compliance
Lightning Source LLC
Chambersburg PA
CBHW031958230426
43672CB00010B/2192